Caldecott on the net

Reading & Internet Activities

Ru Story-Huffman

Alleyside Press®

Fort Atkinson, Wisconsin

Chuck,

*This is for you, because you
are in my heart.*

Published by Alleyside Press,
an imprint of Highsmith Press LLC
W5527 Highway 106
P.O. Box 800
Fort Atkinson, Wisconsin 53538-0800
Fax: 1-920-563-4801
1-800-558-2110

© Copyright by Ru Story-Huffman, 1999
Cover design: Frank Neu

Library of Congress Cataloging-in-Publication Data
  Story-Huffman, Ru, 1959-
    Caldecott on the Net : reading & Internet activities / Ru
  Story-Huffman.
       p.   cm.
    Includes bibliographical references.
    1-57950-020-X (alk. paper)
    1. Children's stories, American--Study and teaching (Elementary)--United
  States--Computer network resources. 2. Children's stories, American--Study
  and teaching (Elementary)--United States. 3. Caldecott Medal--Computer
  network resources. I. Title.
  PS374.C454S77 1999
  025.06 ' 8135099282--dc21   99-36925
                                                                 CIP

Contents

Appendices

HPLink for *Caldecott on the Net*
www.hpress.highsmith.com/rsh1up.htm

Introduction

Our lives changed the day the Internet became accessible to anyone with a computer, modem and a telephone line. Our thoughts, actions and interpretation of the world became more global and more personalized. New experiences became common place and the ability to visit foreign lands, people and cultural events became as simple as a keystroke. Technology is an important part of our lives and the World Wide Web is here to stay. At the same time, many have longed for a return to the simple life, the life that includes the warm memories of reading books with young children. *Caldecott on the Net* is a resource that combines the power of technology and the lure of picture books to explore themes from the selected stories via related websites.

Caldecott Medal Books

The real heart of this book is grounded in the Caldecott Medal books selected for the LearningQuests. Children have long read and loved these stories. Most elementary classrooms and libraries have these award-winning books in their collections. Caldecott Medal books are a tradition in the lives of children, a tradition which pays respect to literature and to a man who recognized the need for quality literature for children. The Caldecott Medal was named in honor of Randolph Caldecott, a nineteenth-century English illustrator of children's books. Established in 1937, the Caldecott Medal is awarded each year to the illustrator of the most distinguished picture book published in America the previous year. To win the Caldecott Medal, an artist has to demonstrate an ability to interpret the story and develop illustrations of excellence in conjunction with the theme. The Caldecott Medal is awarded for illustrations, though other factors are considered. The Medal is sponsored and presented by the Association of Library Service to Children (ALSC), a division of the American Library Association. Winning the Caldecott Medal is a very high honor. Besides the selection of the award-winning book, the Caldecott Medal committee often chooses honor books to be recognized as well.

Often Caldecott Medal books are included in the primary and elementary school curriculum. Illustrations in Caldecott Medal books are of a variety of medium and style. Often Caldecott Medal books are used with an art curriculum or to enhance a given topic of learning. Some books are used on a regular basis by educators for their educational merit. The use of literature in the Whole Language and the Balanced Reading Program methods of teaching offer students the opportunity to learn a concept through the use of literature. Caldecott Medal books have been used to reinforce childhood experiences, thoughts, feelings, and education. Libraries use the Caldecott Medal books in programs for preschool and elementary age children. Often,

Introduction

as with the Newbery Medal books, adults enjoy reading and discussing Caldecott Medal books in library book discussion programs. Most libraries include Caldecott Medal books in their collection development plan, as do school library media centers.

Caldecott on the Net is an effort to enhance the appreciation, study and enjoyment of quality children's literature through the use of the Internet. The Internet has changed and will continue to change our educational system. The Internet can be viewed as a Web; at the center of the Web is the learner. The learner travels different routes or links with different websites to discover specific information. As the learner travels those routes, they are exposed to many other pieces of information, which are often related to the subject at hand.

Using LearningQuests to Expand Reading and Internet Experiences

Caldecott on the Net provides the teacher, librarian and parent the opportunity to expose children to the Internet through the use of Caldecott Medal books. Selected Caldecott Medal winners have been used to develop an educational concept known as a LearningQuest. LearningQuests are based on WebQuests, which were developed by Bernie Dodge at San Diego State University. In short, a WebQuest is an educational activity that uses the Internet to teach children. A WebQuest is an actual mounted Internet Web page that contains specific tasks, questions, processes, and Internet links. Children are provided a scenario and have stated educational activities to complete their goals. *Caldecott on the Net* is designed as a time-saving tool for educators, librarians and parents. The questions, learning goals, Internet sites, extended activities and resources have already been developed and are provided here. Supplementary print and Internet resources are included for use by the educator to extend the learning situation, or for use by librarians as a basis for developing their youth programs.

The concept of *Caldecott on the Net* expands the WebQuest theme for use by a wide audience. Educators and librarians who do not have the time or resources to mount a Web page can use this volume to create a single Web activity or handout. Schools or libraries that do not have the necessary computer hardware to initiate a group learning experience can use the LearningQuests in paper format. The LearningQuests are designed so that students can read from the pages of this book and do the World Wide Web searching using the recommended Internet Uniform Resource Locators (URLs). Websites chosen for inclusion in *Caldecott on the Net* have been selected to best comply with educational standards for children.

Teaching your students just a few Internet basics is necessary before attempting a LearningQuest. Establishing the level of the students' computer literacy will also aid in adapting the suggested activities to meet students' needs. Advice on working with new computer users is presented on page 9. In addition, a LearningQuest template is included at the end of the book (p. 91) and an electronic version of the template has been added to the 🔗Links Web page (p. 10).

If interested in further information on the use of WebQuests, visit the sites listed on the next page, many of which contain additional Internet links.

WebQuests

WebQuests were developed by Bernie Dodge at San Diego State University. For more information, you might try the Web page created by him for WebQuests at:

The WebQuest Page
http://edweb.sdsu.edu/webquest/webquest.html

There are many additional sites with further information:

WebQuests: What Are They?
http://www-education.nmsu.edu:8001/webquest/wq_intro.html

WebQuests in Our Future: The Teacher's Role in Cyberspace
http://www.school.discovery.com/schrockguide/webquest/webquest.html

WebQuests in Our Future: A Slideshow
http://www.school.discovery.com/schrockguide/webquest/wqsl1.html

A WebQuest About WebQuests
http://edweb.sdsu.edu/webquest/webquestwebquest.html

Some Thoughts About WebQuests
http://edweb.sdsu.edu/EdWeb_Folder/courses/EDTEC596/About_WebQuests.html

Using WebQuests in Your Classroom
http://121.ed.psu.edu/linktuts/inteweb.htm

WebQuests Handout
http://gilligan.esu7.k12.ne.us/~esu7web/resources/webqhand.html

WebQuest Resources
http://gilligan.esu7.k12.ne.us/~esu7web/resources/webq.html

WebQuests
http://www.spa3.k12.sc.us/WebQuests.html

WebQuest Template
http://www.esu7.org/~esu7web/resources/wqtemplate.html

Many Internet sites have WebQuests which have been developed by educators. To access available WebQuests on the Net, use the keyword "webquests" in your preferred Internet search engine.

How to Use This Book

Each LearningQuest is a complete, ready-to-use instructional or program resource that works well with individual or group situations. Each LearningQuest is suitable for classroom, library or home use. The LearningQuests contain an introduction of the chosen Caldecott book, an assignment written in terms understandable by the intended age group, Internet resources that can be used to complete the stated activities, and fun things to do which extend the learning process and add to the enjoyment of the entire learning activity. The conclusion provides a wrap-up to the LearningQuest activity and is designed to reinforce gained knowledge. Additional recommended Internet Web pages and literature are provided for the educator, librarian or parent seeking further resources.

The LearningQuests in *Caldecott on the Net* are designed for children in the lower elementary school grades. Many of the Internet activities were chosen, not only for their educational content, but to provide young children practice with keyboarding skills and mouse manipulation.

Caldecott on the Net contains eighteen LearningQuests. Each quest may be mounted on a school or library website using any standard HTML editing software or photocopied as ready-to-use activity sheets. Two versions of the basic LearningQuest template are included starting on page 91. The first is a copy of the template formatted to show how a basic LearningQuest would appear for students. It identifies where the information for the quests should be inserted. The second template includes the HTML (HyperText Markup Language) coding that you can use to create your own Web-ready document. The HTML template is also available on the Web page created for *Caldecott on the Net*, and can be downloaded from <www.hpress.highsmith.com/rsh1up.htm>. These templates can be used to turn the print activities here into Web-ready units or to create additional LearningQuests. If you lack equipment or time, you may prefer to have students work from photocopies of the LearningQuest pages.

Staying Current with 🔗 Links

Obsolescence is a big issue with the Internet. To extend the usefulness of *Caldecott on the Net*, the author will post changes to the 🔗 Links Web page at: www.hpress.highsmith.com/rsh1up.htm>. This page will feature updates on URLs, an electronic listing of Web addresses referenced in the print edition, an HTML-coded copy of the LearningQuest template, and a new quest for future Caldecott winners as they are announced. Internet addresses will be checked on a regular basis to ensure availability. In addition, opportunity will be provided for your reaction and comments on the use of *Caldecott on the Net* in the classroom, library or home. A goal of *Caldecott on the Net* is to provide teachers, librarians, and parents with an ongoing resource of educational opportunities available on the World Wide Web. This page will be maintained as long as the book is available.

Working with New Computer Users

If children are unfamiliar with computers and the Internet, the following steps are recommended:

Introduce the students to the following basic computer skills, either individually or in small groups. Demonstrate each step, and then ask each student to repeat them. Stress the importance of seeking the assistance of a teacher or librarian if they forget these procedures or they experience any problems.

- How to turn on the computer.
- If the computer is password protected, review the use of the password and the reason for security, as well as the computer log-on procedure.
- Explain the computer's menu, and what the icons represent.
- Demonstrate how to use the computer's mouse to access specific programs.
- Demonstrate how to exit a program, log-out, and turn off the computer.

The next day, ask the students to repeat these procedures. Continue to repeat this process until each student has mastered these basic steps.

After the students have mastered the basic computer skills, introduce them to the Internet and the World Wide Web, using the following steps:

- Explain that the Internet is a network of computers, and that the World Wide Web provides access to a "library" of information resources. Note that a browser permits a computer user to locate and access specific "sites" or pages on the Web, and that each of these pages has an "address" called a Uniform Resource Locator (URL).
- Show the students how to use the computer's modem to access the Internet. Explain that a modem is required to access the Internet using telephone lines. If a password and specific log-on procedure is required, demonstrate how that is done.
- Once you have connected to the library's or school's Internet Provider using the computer modem, demonstrate how to locate a specific website using the computer's browser.
- Be very careful to explain that not every website on the Internet is appropriate for children, and they should only use URLs that have been recommended for them, such as the Web sites included in this book.
- Let them search for specific sites using sample URLs contained in this book. Explain the importance of using the exact URL, and demonstrate what happens the URL is incorrectly keyed.
- Demonstrate how to log out of the Internet and exit the modem. If your school or library does not have unlimited access to the Internet, explain the importance of logging in and out as soon as the search has been completed.

Repeat this procedure on the following day, and on succeeding days until all students have mastered these basic steps.

Website Evaluation and Selection Criteria

The Web has many "authors" including educational institutions, governments, private industry, profit and nonprofit corporations and everyday people. It is within these pages that the learner is exposed to all types of information. Critical thinking is an important tool for students to possess. The Internet can aid in the development of critical thinking, higher order reasoning and discrimination of sources. Deciding authenticity of information presented is important when using the Internet to educate and entertain children. When librarians, teachers, and parents choose literature for children, they use certain criteria to aid in that selection. When finding Internet sites for use in an educational setting, having an understanding of the information presented is very important. To aid in the selection of Internet resources, the following concepts should be considered before any website is recommended for students to use.

Authorship: You can get some ideas about authorship from the domain name, but often finding the real source of the information is difficult.

◆ Is the author or authoring organization provided? Who is the "author" of the Internet site? It is a college or university? Government? Corporation? A personal homepage?

◆ Is the source of the information given? (This information should be available from the site author on request if it is not given on the site.)

Purpose: Each site on the Web has a purpose for existing, these include informing and educating, but also selling, persuading and misinforming.

◆ Does the page provide a statement about its sponsorship and purpose?

◆ Is there advertising? Does it detract from the other site content?

◆ If authorship and purpose are not stated, is there a bias in the presentation?

Content: Answers to the questions above will help to evaluate issues of bias and quality. Some other issues to consider about the content include:

◆ Does the Internet Web page meet the needs of stated educational goals, curricula, and standards?

◆ Will the information contained educate and entertain the children?

◆ Is there too much information presented which may frustrate the young learner?

◆ Is there information included which does not pertain to your subject, or would be harmful in some way to children?

◆ Is the Internet page age appropriate for the audience? Is it too advanced for the intended grade or age level.

Currency: A major problem with the Internet is obsolescence. Websites have a tendency to disappear. Information found on Internet Web pages can be relevant one day and outdated the next. Or you may be looking at information that hasn't been reviewed or updated in a couple of years.

◆ When was this page last updated? Is the information presented out-of-date? Was new information added at the last updating?

◆ Are there any inactive links included in the Internet sites? If you find links to other information that are inactive or outdated, you can assume the initial site has not been thoroughly checked.

Design: Consider the overall design of the page for information clarity and presentation.

◆ Has the site been designed so that you can move through it easily and quickly to find the information desired?

◆ Is the page fun to use; will children find the presentation stimulating or entertaining when visiting the page?

◆ Are there too many graphics, or are the graphics so large the page is slow to load?

◆ Is the page hard to decipher?

Ease-of-Use: A Web page that is difficult to use may provide a frustrating experience for children and adults.

◆ Is the Internet site easy to search?

◆ Is the search engine or mechanism easy to manipulate, or do they pose possible problems for children?

Evaluation Resources

Evaluation of Internet sites is a growing concern. The Internet itself features some evaluation criteria websites. To further your understanding of the criteria used in selecting Web pages for educational use, visit these sites:

Critical Evaluations Surveys
http://www.school.discovery.com/schrockguide/eval.html

CyberGuides: A Rating System
http://www.cyberbee.com/guides.html

The ABC's of Website Evaluation
http://school.discovery.com/schrockguide/ppoint.html
Choose "ABC's of Web Site Evaluation" in the PowerPoint format to view a presentation developed for educators on web page evaluation.

Selection Criteria
http://www.ala.org/parentspage/greatsites/criteria.html

Evaluating Web Resources
http://www2.widener.edu/Wolfgram-Memorial-Library/webeval.htm

Teachers' CyberGuide
http://www.cyberbee.com/guide1.html

Internet Curriculum #3: Evaluation of a Web Page
http://www.school.discovery.com/schrockguide/brush/intles3.html

The Good, the Bad, and the Ugly
http://lib.nmsu.edu/staff/susabeck/eval.html

As with any information, careful evaluation can save time, energy, and provide the best learning situation possible. Evaluation of the Internet and the information presented will aid in the instructional design for all computer-aided instruction.

In Summary

Children are exposed to computers at a very young age. Many preschool children can grasp the concepts of simple computer games and activities. *Caldecott on the Net* is designed to introduce computer skills, increase awareness of information and entertain young children. At the same time, children will be exposed to quality children's literature, which can aid in the development of necessary reading skills. The American Association of School Librarians (AASL) and the Association for Education Communications and Technology (AECT) have developed *Information Literacy Standards for Student Learning*, which provides a framework and stated goals for improving student use of computers, the Internet, and other educational technology.[1] *Caldecott on the Net* was written to contribute to these goals through activities that are clear, understandable, and enjoyable.

Although *Caldecott on the Net* stresses the Internet and educational technology, literature is a vital aspect of this volume. The Internet exposes children to new ideas, thoughts and information. As do books, which have long been a part of our lives, and will continue to influence us. Through books, children and adults have been educated, entertained, enlightened and enriched. We use books in a variety of situations, and Caldecott Medal books represent children's books held in high esteem by children and adults. Those who use *Caldecott on the Net* in the classroom, library and home have the opportunity to continue the time honored tradition of quality literature, accompanied with the resources of the electronic frontier.

Notes

1. American Association of School Librarians/Association for Educational Communications and Technology. *Information Literacy Standards for Student Learning*. Chicago, ALA, 1998.

Caldecott LearningQuest

Introduction

The Caldecott Medal is given to the illustrator of a children's book. An illustrator is someone who draws or paints the pictures found in your favorite books. Winning the Caldecott Medal is a high honor.

Assignment

During this LearningQuest, you will learn about the Caldecott Medal and see some winning books. You will also read about some of the books that have won the Caldecott Medal.

Internet Resources

Reading Corner - Caldecotts

http://ccpl.carr.lib.md.us/read/caldecott.htm *Activities 1 & 2*

Caldecott Medal Winners, 1938–1998

http://www.ala.org/alsc/cquick.html *Activities 3 & 4*

Activities

1. What color is the seal on the cover of a Caldecott Medal book?

2. Click on the button for "1990s" and then click the cover of the book *Officer Buckle and Gloria*. Who wrote and illustrated this book? What year did this book win the Caldecott Medal?

3. What was the title of the 1998 Caldecott Medal book?

4. Who illustrated this book?

Fun Things to Do

It might be fun to gather some Caldecott Medal books from your school or public library. There is a complete list of these books located at the following web page:

www.ala.org/alsc/cquick.html. Find five titles and read them with your classmates, or have your teacher, librarian or parent read them to you. Since the Caldecott Medal is awarded for illustrations, choose your favorite book based on the pictures. Share with the class why you chose the book you did.

Conclusion

Winning the Caldecott Medal is a great honor. Many schools, libraries and homes have Caldecott Medal books in the collection. Often schools and libraries have all the medal winning books! Reading a Caldecott Medal book is fun because you get to read a great story told with wonderful art!

Educator Notes

The following websites provide information for adults to use in the education of children. Some provide the award criteria for use with the medal, others present a bibliography of all medal-winning books. Each website can be adapted for use with children in grades K–2.

Websites

Caldecott Medal Home Page

http://www.ala.org/alsc/caldecott.html

This is the home page of the Caldecott Medal, sponsored by the Association for Library Services to Children, a division of the American Library Association. Each year this site is updated to provide information on the new medal book and honor books.

Caldecott Medal Winners, 1938–1999

http://www.ala.org/alsc/cquick.html

Each Caldecott Medal-winning book is listed. Included is the author's name if different than the illustrator, year the award was won and publisher of the selected title. This is a nice printable list which can be used in a variety of ways.

The Randolph Caldecott Medal

http://www.ala.org/alsc/cmedal.html

This page presents a history of the Caldecott Medal, which can be adapted for use with younger children. Also included are criteria for awarding the Caldecott Medal to deserving illustrators.

Caldecott Medal

http://www.calgary.ca/~dkbrown/caldecott.html

Part of The Children's Literature Web Guide, this site provides a complete list of Caldecott Medal and Honor Books, medal history and criteria. The Children's Literature Web Guide is an excellent resource for the study of children's literature.

The Caldecott Medal

http://ils.unc.edu/award/chome.html

This is a nice site that lists information about the Caldecott Medal. Links are provided to the American Library Association and the Randolph Caldecott Society of America.

Caldecott Medal Books

http://www.story-house.com/award/calde.html

This page has links to the criteria, origin of the medal, and a description of the medal. This page also offers a searchable list of Caldecott Medal books with short synopses and grade level information. Story-house.com is a commercial site which sells children's books.

Randolph Caldecott Society of America

http://macserver.stjohns.k12.fl.us/others/rc.html

Providing biographical information on Randolph Caldecott, this site is helpful for educators and librarians looking for in-depth information about Randolph Caldecott. A list of books illustrated by Caldecott is included.

Books

The following books offer teaching strategies and classroom/library enrichment ideas for use with Caldecott Medal books.

Association of Library Service to Children. *The Newbery and Caldecott Awards: A Guide to the Medal and Honor Books*. American Library Association, 1998. Each medal and honor book is presented with a synopsis and full bibliographic information. The educator who wishes to find a Caldecott book to meet a specific teaching need would find this book useful.

Brown, Muriel W. *Newbery and Caldecott Medalists and Honor Book Winners: Bibliographies and Resource Material Through 1991*. Neal-Schuman, 1992. This is a second edition of an earlier work by Jim Roginski, which covered titles to 1978. Included in this title are background reading and primary and secondary titles for each author and illustrator.

Englebaugh, Debi. *Art Through Children's Literature: Creative Art Lessons for Caldecott Books*. Teacher Ideas Press, 1994. Caldecott Medal books are a natural extension for art lessons. The illustrations are varied and the techniques used are inspiring. This book provides art lessons which have been based on Caldecott Medal winners.

Hamm, Jody. *Latch on to Literature: A Teacher's Guide to 12 Caldecott Medal & Honor Books*. Highsmith Press, 1993. Twelve Caldecott medal and honor books published between 1965 and 1990 have been chosen for use in the classroom.

Marcus, Leonard S. *A Caldecott Celebration: Six Artists and Their Paths to the Caldecott Medal*. Walker, 1998. In honor of the 60th anniversary of the Caldecott Medal, this book has been produced by Marcus, a noted children's book historian. The six Caldecott Medal winners included are Robert McCloskey, Marcia Brown, Maurice Sendak, William Steig, Chris Van Allsburg, and David Wiesner.

Moen, Christine Boardman. *Teaching With Caldecott Books: Activities Across the Curriculum*. Scholastic, 1994. A whole-language/critical thinking approach is taken in this book, which uses Caldecott books as a curriculum base. Fifteen Caldecott books have been chosen to promote instructional activities.

LQ2

Where the Wild Things Are

Maurice Sendak

Harper, 1963 • Caldecott Medal, 1964

Introduction

After Max is sent to bed without any supper, he travels to the land of the "wild things." Max tames the wild things and becomes their king, but he still longs to be at home instead.

Assignment

Read the story *Where the Wild Things Are,* or have your teacher read it to the class. In this story, you will meet some "wild things." Dinosaurs and monsters are considered by some to be "wild things." During this activity, you will meet some dinosaurs and monsters. You will also have some fun!

Internet Resources

Animated Bagel Maker 1

http://www.acekids.com/bagels1.htm   *Activity 1*

Dinosaurs

http://nyelabs.kcts.org/teach/episodeguides/eg03.html   *Activity 2*
(Macromedia Flash needed to access the full website.)

Creature Crazy

http://www.pbs.org/kratts/crazy/madlibs/index.html   *Activity 3*

Build-a-Monster

http://www.rahul.net/renoir/monster/index.html   *Activity 4*

Create-a-Saurus

http://www.kidspace.com/kids/dinosaurs/createasaurus   *Activity 5*

Coloring!

http://coloring.com/demo/begin.cdc?img=dragon   *Activity 6*

Activities

1. Bagels are fun to eat, but more fun to make into silly monsters! Using your mouse, scroll toward the bottom of the page until you see the words, "The Incredible Bagel Maker." Pick the following information for your bagel, and see what happens.

   Is your bagel a boy or a girl?

   What is your favorite bagel flavor?

   What type of hair will your bagel have?

   What will its eyes look like?

   Does your bagel wear shoes?

2. How much did the largest dinosaur weigh? How long was this dinosaur? What was this dinosaur called?

3. Choose one of the adventures and fill in the blanks to explore the creatures you can create. If you have questions, ask an adult. (*Educator note: You can tailor this activity to your specific age group by choosing the appropriate level of activity.*)

4. It is time to build a monster. Use your mouse to click on a body part and see how your monster changes.

5. Let's create our own dinosaur by clicking on patterns and dinosaur shapes.

6. Choose your colors wisely. Dragons like to look nice.

Fun Things to Do

Draw a picture of one of the creatures that you made in "Build a Monster." Did your monster have a frog's head or feet? Did it have legs or hands? Use crayons to create your monster and then share it with your class. What is your monster's name? Where does your monster live? What does your monster like to eat?

Conclusion

Monsters and dinosaurs can be fun and exciting. But, just like Max learned in the story *Where the Wild Things Are*, sometimes the best place to be is at home.

Educator Notes

The following Internet sites and books can provide the educator with addition information, activities and curriculum extenders.

Coloring.Com

http://coloring.com/choose.html

At this Internet site, children can color a variety of pictures, including a dragon, snake or unicorn. Children will gain experience at using the mouse by clicking on a color and transferring that color to the picture. They will also have practice in identifying colors.

LearningQuest 2 : Where the Wild Things Are

Dino Design Board

http://www.afroam.org/children/fun/dino/dino.html

Designed as a site for young children, all who visit here will enjoy this dinosaur activity. Shockwave plug-in is needed to play this game, in which participants make their own dinosaur. A child may end up the head of a Tyrannosaurus or body of a flying dinosaur. And while kids are constructing their crazy creatures, they gain experience at using the mouse to move items on-screen. For those who do not have Shockwave, this site features a link for information on obtaining the necessary plug-in.

The Dinosaur Interplanetary Gazette

http://www.users.interport.net/~dinosaur/saurofindo.html

For the ultimate dinosaur enthusiast, this site provides information, graphics, stories, links, books, school reports and much more. This page is produced by Laser Publishing Group, who promote themselves as a publisher of educational websites.

Dinosauria On-Line

http://www.dinosauria.com

This fun site features all types of information about dinosaurs. The picture gallery would be a nice addition to a unit of study on dinosaurs. Some of the links may be a bit advanced for younger children, but teachers, librarians and parents will be able to pull information appropriate for their target age group.

Kendra's Coloring Book

http://www.geocitites.com/EnchantedForest/7155/robot.html

What's more fun than coloring a robot? Internet coloring books are fun, educational and provide children practice in hand-eye coordination and in computer skills.

MindsEye Monster Exchange

http://www.win4edu.com/minds-eye/monster.html

This classroom Internet project encourages children to use the computer to describe a monster, thus reinforcing language arts skills. Students then draw the wildest monster they can imagine and the description of their monster is e-mailed to a partner school. The children in the other school then draw the monster, based upon the description of the originating school. A Web page is featured at this site which shows the monsters and descriptions by students in primary and above.

Monsters by Kristen

http://www.monsters.net/

This is a site of games which feature monsters. Most of the games do not require a special plug-in. There are little green monsters dancing, a monster movie and monster fashion show. Children will have fun with this site and enjoy the variety of monsters and their antics.

Monsters, Monsters, Monsters

http://www.2cyberlinks.com/monster.html

This is another activity which introduces primary students to the Internet through an e-mail project. Students are provided a description and can develop their own version of a monster. The results are then shared with other project participants and the world via the World Wide Web. The developer of this project is a teacher in Florida.

Sticker Book

http://www.kidspace.com/kids/sticker

By clicking on a sticker from the sticker book and then clicking the drawing where they want to place the sticker, children can make some pretty "wild looking things." This activity gives practice with the mouse and provides a creative experience for young children.

Books

Angelilli, Chris. ***Dr. Skincrawl's Creepy Creatures: With 3-D Glasses.*** Golden Books Family Entertainment, 1997. Another book in the Screamin' 3-D Series, this book features creepy creatures, which with the accompaniment of the 3-D glasses, become even "creepier!"

Big & Small Dinosaurs. Modern Publishing, 1997. This book is a picture book, which doubles as an activity and coloring book. Children in grades K–3 will enjoy the pictures of dinosaurs which they can color. They will also learn about different dinosaurs and what those dinosaurs looked like.

Dunham, Laura. ***Draw Your Own Monsters.*** Price Stern Sloan, 1997. For the child who likes to draw, this book is ideal. Even the youngest child can have fun drawing the monsters included here. *Draw Your Own Monsters* would also benefit those who like to look at monsters and make up stories about them.

Griffith, Helen V. ***Dinosaur Habitat.*** Greenwillow, 1998. Children in grades K–2 will enjoy this book, which features dinosaurs and their habitat. It would be useful in a science class, in which students are studying dinosaurs or the habitat of creatures on our planet.

Phillips, Louis. ***Ask Me Anything About Monsters.*** Avon, 1997. A nonfiction "question and answer" book, *Ask Me Anything About Monsters* would be a good book for children who like monsters and like to ask questions. This book is intended for children ages eight to twelve, but could be adapted for use with primary-aged children.

Rosenbluth, Roz. ***Boo Goes There?: With 3-D Glasses.*** Golden Books Family Entertainment, 1997. This book, illustrated by Peter Fasolino, features a fun look at monsters. Part of the Screamin' 3-D Series, children will enjoy the variety of monsters found here.

White Snow, Bright Snow

Illustrated by Roger Duvoisin
Written by Alvin Tresselt

Lothrop, 1947 • Caldecott Medal, 1948

Introduction

During the snow storm, the adults are busy preparing for the white world. The children are enjoying the fun that comes with a snow storm. Eventually, the snow melts and the flowers of spring appear.

Assignment

When it snows, the colors of our world become covered in white. Trees are white, the ground is white and the streets are white. After the snow melts and spring appears, the colors return brighter than before. Through this activity you will learn about colors and their importance in our world.

Internet Resources

Crayola Trivia

  http://www.crayola.com/funfacts/trivia1.html   *Activity 1*

How Are Crayons Made?

  http://www.crayola.com/assembly/how_crayon.html   *Activity 2*

Crayola History

  http://www.crayola.com/history/history.html   *Activities 3 & 4*

Color with PBS Kids

  http://www.pbs.org/kids/fungames/coloring   *Activity 5*

Activities

1. This is an exciting trivia game. Read each question and choose an answer using your computer mouse. After each question, you'll see the correct answer. How well do you know the history of colors?

2. What two things are used to make crayons?

3. What is the name of the company that makes Crayola colors?

4. When did Crayola celebrate its 90th birthday? What were three new color names that were introduced that same year?

5. Pick a character from your favorite television show and begin the fun! Choose from *Arthur, Mister Roger's Neighborhood, Storytime, Adventures from the Book of Virtues* or *The P-Pals* to name a few. You can print out coloring pages using your printer, or color them right on the computer screen.

Fun Things to Do

Use the following Internet site to read some poems about colors:

Crayola Poems

> http://www.bri-dge.com/poems/poem272.html

After you've read the poems, write your own poem about your favorite color. Is it a silly poem, or a poem which describes something? Share your poem with your class.

Conclusion

Colors are all around us. We see colors in our homes, schools, libraries and world. Each day, the colors remind us of the variety we have in our lives.

Educator notes

There are a lot of coloring books, pictures, and information about colors and art on the Internet. The following sites are a sampling of those available on the Web.

Art Education — Kids Rule!

> http://www.hukilau.com/kidsrule

> The lessons presented at this Internet site are intended to help the youngest child identify colors, be creative and expressive. This searchable Internet site features a variety of art activities for children grades K–12, art tutorials and lessons.

Color Garden

> http://www.eduplace.com/rdg/gen_act/color/garden.html

> A science/art activity in which children learn about the variety of colors represented in flowers. The activity includes identification of flowers and colors, an art activity and options for teachers. This site is from Houghton Mifflin Education Place, an Internet resource for teachers, parents, librarians and children.

Cool Crafts for Kids

> http://www.crayola.com

> The home page for Crayola Company, this page features a coloring book, craft area for kids, game room, and a teacher's help section. Also included is a special place for parents. This site is a nice site for education and entertainment.

LearningQuest 3 : White Snow, Bright Snow

Crayola Family Play

http://www.familyplay.com/

Each day new activities and features are added to this Internet site. Designed for use by families, the activities and games are easily adaptable for classroom or library use. Users can browse from the many topics, including arts and crafts, car games or science. In addition, a customized search can be done for specific age levels and skills.

Light and Color

http://nyelabs.kcts.org/teach/episodeguides/eg16.html

Bill Nye, the Science Guy is a popular science program on public television. In this episode, Bill Nye talks about colors, presenting facts, information, and science experiments for children. The episodeguide listed here is accessible without plug-ins. However, to see the interactive parts of this website, plug-ins are needed. MacroMedia Flash is needed to enter the website through the home page.

Shades of Blue

http://www.eduplace.com/rdg/gen_act/color/shades.html

Colors come in a variety of shades and hues. In this activity from the Education Place, teachers have the necessary outline for an unit on recognizing color and shade. This activity is useful as an art activity and can be adapted for use in a library or home.

Teaching Children Colors

http://www.contrib.andrew.cmu.edu/usr/fr0c/TeachColors-E-Book.html

This site is intended for adults, and provides a short introduction to helping children learn to identify colors. Specifically, hues and shades are discussed and tips are provided on helping children learn to distinguish between the subtle shades of a color.

TeacherView: The Rainbow Fish

http://www.eduplace.com/tview/tviews/levine31.html

Another selection from the Education Place, this activity features teacher-created units which are based on books. In *The Rainbow Fish*, three themes are presented, one of which is an unit about colors. Additional books can be found at: www.eduplace.com/tview/index.html.

Books

Color. Scholastic, 1997. This book, intended for children in K–5, will aid in the discovery and identification of color. The wide age level of this book makes it a good choice for use in a large group setting with a variety of age groups represented.

Colors on the Farm. Modern Publishing, 1996. This book features stickers which aid in recognizing colors. Using the theme of a "farm," children are invited to learn their colors in a picture-book format. The farm theme will lead to a good learning opportunity and enjoyment by children.

Fowler, Allan. *All the Colors of the Rainbow.* Children's Press, 1998. Nature, color, and weather combined to offer children information on the composition of a rainbow's colors.

Riley, Peter D. *Light and Colors.* (Straightforward Science Series) Franklin Watts, 1999. This book is intended to teach children about the science of color and light.

Schroeder, Pamela, and Jean M. Donisch. *Colors.* Rourke, 1996. Learning to identify colors is a big step in the lives of young children. This book, designed for the youngest children, presents familiar objects and the colors they are associated with. *Colors* is part of the What's the Big Idea? series.

A Story, A Story

Gail E. Haley

Atheneum, 1970 • Caldecott Medal, 1971

Introduction

The great African spider man, Kwaku Ananse, tries to win the Sky God's box of stories so he can share them with the world. In order to win the stories, Kwaku Anase must complete three difficult tasks.

Assignment

Storytelling is a fun way to learn. Through stories, we can learn about others, learn how things are done and have fun, all at the same time. We are all storytellers. Now it is time for you to learn about storytelling and share some stories with your class.

Internet Resources

Wendy's World of Stories for Children
> http://www.wendy.com/children/ *Activities 1 & 2*

Funny You Should Ask
> http://pbs.org/kids/fungames/fysa/fysa.htm *Activity 3*

Internet Public Library Story Hour
> http://www.ipl.org/youth/StoryHour *Activity 4* (requires sound)

Activities

1. What is a fable? Who wrote many fables? What is the title of one of those fables?

2. What is a folk tale? Where did folk tales come from? What is the title of a folk tale?

3. Fill in the blanks for a fun, silly story. After you've completed your story, read it and print the story. Share your story with your class.

4. Listen to two stories from this Internet site. Which story was your favorite.

LearningQuest 4 : A Story, A Story

Fun Things to Do

Go to the following Internet site:

http://pbs.org/kcet/storytime/color1.htm

Print the picture from this site and color it using crayons or magic markers. Make up a story about what the boy is doing in the picture and share your story with your class members. Be sure to give your boy a name and tell a little about him, such as his age or the things he likes to do. You'll find yourself becoming a storyteller!

Conclusion

Storytelling is a fun activity that everyone can enjoy. There are a lot of great stories in the library and on the Internet. Through this activity, we've had the opportunity to learn new stories and share stories with our classmates and friends.

Educator Notes

Storytelling had its origins in the oral tradition. Today, the Internet has taken that oral tradition a step further with the following sites:

The Art of Story Telling

http://www.seanet.com/~eldrbarry/roos/art.htm

This extensive, personal Web page has much useful information on storytelling. Included are links for effective storytelling tips for the beginner, books on storytelling, articles on storytelling, and storytelling resources available via the World Wide Web. There are also links for Web pages of storytellers, storytelling organizations and listserves on storytelling. Much information can be gained through this Internet site by the novice or professional who uses storytelling in any situation.

Arthur's Stories

http://www.pbs.org/wgbh/arthur/arthur/stories/index.html

Arthur the Aardvark is a character from a series of children's books by Marc Brown. Arthur also has his own show on PBS. Through this site, children can meet Arthur and his friends and family, have fun and submit their own stories for inclusion on the site.

Bedtime Story

http://the-office.com/bedtime-story

This site is a collection of stories that are suitable for sharing with children of all ages. Included are stories about children and their pets, magical creatures and funny stories. The stories included in this Internet site could be used at home, school or library, and offer enjoyment for all.

Children's Literature -- Resources for Storytellers

http://www.acs.ucalgary.ca/~dkbrown/rstory.html

This page is from the Children's Literature Web Guide, an excellent resource for all aspects of children's literature. The Resources for Storytellers provides links for story resources, puppetry, folklore, discussion groups and library storytime resources. Though there are just a handful of Web page links provided, this is a valuable resource.

My Favorite Book

http://www.pbs.org/kcet/storytime/color3.htm

Print this page and children can draw a picture from their favorite book, the dust jacket or a picture of a book character. This page is a good page to spark a book discussion or can be used to create a bulletin board or classroom decoration.

Reading Tips

http://www.pbs.org/kcet/storytime/readtipe.htm

The time spent reading books can lead to a storytelling session between child and adult. Often the two will talk about what they have read and discuss situations. This Internet site has valuable information for all adults who have contact with children. Reading tips, getting children involved in the reading process and selecting books are a few of the helpful topics covered.

Story Starters

http://ericir.syr.edu/Virtual/Lessons/Lang_arts/Story_telling/STT0001.html

This ERIC document is the result of a teacher's workshop on using story starters in the classroom. In this lesson plan, children are provided props which they use to help them make up a story. Included are objectives, resources, procedures and variations of the lessons. For the teacher or librarian who wishes to encourage children to tell stories, this lesson provides a good beginning.

Storybox

http://www.dreambox.com/storybox/storybox.shtml

Original stories which children can read and respond to. Children can click through the pages of the story, practicing computer and reading skills at the same time.

Storyteller.net

http://storyteller.net

A site intended for adults, Storyteller.net presents information on storytelling , the oral tradition and has a weekly story from storytellers around the country. Use this site to find stories for classroom or library use or to get information about storytellers and stories.

Storytelling

http://www.motell.org/telling.htm

The history and use of storytelling is presented for adults at this site, but the information can be adapted for use with children through second grade. Included are links for storytelling resources, stories and upcoming storytelling events. This site is a presentation of MO-Tell, a Missouri storytelling association.

Storytelling, Drama, Creative Dramatics, Puppetry & Readers Theater for Children & Young Adults

http://falcon.jmu.edu/~ramseyil/drama.htm

Interpretation of literature can be done a variety of ways, and this site provides information on many aspects of storytelling and creative dramatic techniques. There are five categories, which are mentioned in the title of this Web page. Each category provides numerous links to information, techniques, story festivals, articles, and other resources. For the teacher or librarian who is interested in any or all of these storytelling techniques, this site is an excellent choice.

Storytelling in the Elementary Classroom

http://www.indiana.edu/~eric_rec/ieo/bibs/story.html

This website is an ERIC document which provides citations and links to the topic of storytelling in the classroom. Included are Internet sites and citations from the ERIC database. The list does not cover all the material available via ERIC or the Internet, rather is an introduction to the subject. Much information can be gained on the educational value of storytelling in the elementary classroom through the use of the sites and articles listed on this Web page.

Storytelling with the Flannel Board

http://falcon.jmu.edu/~ramseyil/flannel.htm

The flannel board is an excellent tool for use in storytelling. This Internet site provides information on creating the story, flannelboard materials, stories for use with a flannel board and a bibliography of professional literature for teacher, librarian or parent. For those who have little or no experience with the flannel board, this site provides a good start. Those who are experienced may find new stories or books on the subject to add to their storytelling list.

Storytime Coloring Page

http://www.pbs.org/kcet/storytime/coloring.htm

The coloring pages at this site all reflect reading. Children can print the pages and color the images. Also included are links for games, book lists and resources for adults, including many of interest to educators.

Topic of the Week

http://www.pbs.org/kids/babbleon/getreal/real.htm

Each week a scenario is presented and children can write their own responses and post them out on the World Wide Web. In addition, children can read the responses written by other children. Not only does this Internet site illustrate storytelling, it provides practice in creative writing.

The Wizard of Oz

http://seamonkey.ed.asu.edu/oz/wizard1.html

The classic tale *The Wizard of Oz* is retold by kindergarten and first grade children in Arizona. Included are illustrations produced by the children. Used as an example for educators, this website illustrates the variety of activities which can be created when combining literature and technology.

Books

Duke, Kate. ***Aunt Isabel Tells a Good One.*** Dutton Children's, 1992. Kate Duke is a children's author who likes to use animals in her stories, and this book is no exception. Children K–2 will enjoy Isabel and her stories.

Huff, Mary Jo. ***Storytelling with Puppets, Preps & Playful Tales***. Monday Morning, 1998. This book is intended for the teacher, librarian or parent of young children, who is interested in storytelling using props. The props included in this book should aid in the enjoyment and learning experience of the intended audience.

Marsh, Valerie. ***Paper-Cutting Stories from A to Z.*** Highsmith Press, 1992. Paper-cutting is one of the variety of ways to tell a story. The author has created 26 easy-to-tell stories, one for each letter of the alphabet. Ideal for PK–2.

Pellowski, Anne. ***The Storytelling Handbook: A Young People's Collection of Unusual Tales & Helpful Hints on How to Tell Them.*** Simon & Schuster Children's, 1995. Anne Pellowski is known for her work with storytelling, and in this book she addresses younger audiences. Designed for children ages eight and up, this book can be adapted for use with younger children and includes information that can be used in a classroom to present storytelling and folklore.

Schecter, Ellen. ***Sleep Tight, Pete.*** Bantam, 1995. Pete snuggles while his mom creates bedtime stories in which he is the star. Designed children who are beginning to read independently. *Sleep Tight* will build confidence in their new reading skills.

A Tree Is Nice

Illustrated by Marc Simont
Written by Janice Udry

Harper, 1956 • Caldecott Award, 1957

Introduction

Trees are all over our world and provide us with many things. Trees give us shade, a place for cats to hide and children to play. Trees are very, very nice.

Assignment

In this LearningQuest, you will find out about trees and play some games. You will also get to write your own story about a forest.

Internet Resources

Smokey Bear Home Page

> http://www.smokeybear.com/hom.html *Activity 1*

Smokey Bear - Forest Fun

> http://www.smokeybear.com/for.html *Activities 2 & 3*

Smokey Bear - Campfire Games - Amazing Mazes

> http://www.smokeybear.com/cgi-bin/rbox/fr.cgi?mp=cam *Activity 4*

Smokey Bear - Color It

> http://www.smokeybear.com/cgi-bin/rbox/color_it.cgi *Activity 5*

Activities

1. How many acres of forest are there in the United States?

2. What are three things that trees provide us?

3. What is one of the greatest threats to trees in the forest?

4. Play the Amazing Maze game, to find the words "Only you can prevent forest fires." Read the directions provided for playing instructions before you start.

5. Choose a picture from this site and print it out. Using your best coloring skills complete the picture.

Fun Things to Do

Using the following Internet site:

http://www.smokeybear.com/f_for_story_maker.html

It is time for you to write a story! Fill in the blanks with your choice of words and press the submit button. Read you story out loud to your class members, or have your teacher read it to you. Have fun!

Conclusion

Trees are very important. From trees we get lumber, paper, and shade. Not only people like trees, but animals do too, especially Smokey the Bear!

Educator Notes

Trees are very important. The following Internet sites and books can help extend the activities found in this LearningQuest.

Arbor Day History

http://www.ipm.iastate.edu/ipm/hortnews/1993/4-28-1993/arbor.html

An all-text history of Arbor Day is presented at this Internet site. Though written for high school level and adults, some of the information can be used with younger children, such as when the first Arbor Day was held or the name of the founder of Arbor Day.

Bill Nye Episode Guide: Forests

http://nyelabs.kcts.org/teach/episodeguides/eg35.html

Bill Nye the Science Guy is presented on Public Television and enjoyed by all ages. This Internet site lists forestry facts and books on forests. The episodeguide listed here is accessible without plug-ins. However, to see the interactive parts of this website, plug-ins are needed. MacroMedia Flash is needed to enter the website through the home page.

Family.com Activities

http://family.go.com/Categories/Activities/

The Disney Online site has numerous activities, including the two following sites. Picking "Outdoors" from the drop-down topic menu provides activities such as "Forest Crowns and Bracelets," "Maple Seedling Olympics" or "Leaf Pressing."

Forest Glossary

http://family.go.com/Categories/Education/Features/family_1998_04/famf/famf48woods/famf48woods6.html

A forest is made of many layers and this Internet site explains the various layers in terms that children can understand. Educators could use this site as a basis for a vocabulary assignment or to reinforce understanding of forestry concepts.

Web of Life

http://family.go.com/Categories/Education/Features/family_1998_04/famf/famf48woods/famf48woods2.html

This is a game which explores the roles of plants and animals in the forest. The game uses very simple materials and can be played indoors or outdoors by children of all ages.

LearningQuest 5 : A Tree Is Nice

The Freakies Tree

http://www.freakies.com/line_tree.htm

Print and color the tree, which features "Freakies." Freakies are funny animals which may or may not live in trees!

Memory Busters

http://www.smokeybear.com/f_cam_mem.html

This is a memory game with clues about items you would see in a forest. A very quick "peek" is given of the placement of items before they are covered. As with all memory games, this one will teach children memorization skills, object recognition and has the added bonus of providing practice with a computer mouse.

Teaching Youth about Trees

http://www.arborday.org/teaching/teaching.asp?event=

Another page from the National Arbor Day Foundation that directs you to hands-on curriculum kits, booklets, information packets and posters. The information found via these links will benefit a study unit on trees by providing the educator with resources, information and ideas for use in the classroom.

What and When Is Arbor Day?

http://www.arborday.org/what/what.asp?event=

For the child who wants to know information about Arbor Day, this site would be of good use. Three short paragraphs provide an overview on the topic, with links to other aspects of Arbor Day, including how it can be celebrated.

What Kind of Tree Is It?

http://www.domtar.com/arbre/english/questio.htm

There are ten multiple choice questions on this Internet site which test tree identification skills. Children are provided a picture of a tree or leaf and asked to identify the tree. This site would be fun to incorporate into a tree unit for the classroom.

Books

Dorros, Arthur. **A Tree Is Growing**. Scholastic, 1997. This book provides information on how a tree grows. As a resource, A Tree is Growing would aid a unit on the life span of our trees.

Helfrich, Banks. **1-2-3 Tree.** Tossed Salad Production, 1995. Young children through the second grade will benefit from the information on trees presented here. Suitable for classroom or library use.

Oppenheim, Joanne F. **Have You Seen Trees?** Scholastic, 1995. Once again, Scholastic as produced a book which will work well in the classroom, library or home. Young children through grade 2 will benefit from this volume as the information is presented on a level they can comprehend.

Prevost, John F. **Apple Trees.** Abdo & Daughters, 1996. This book specifically pertains to apple trees and teaches about this versatile member of our forest family. Children, especially those who enjoy apples, will like learning about how the apples grow on trees.

Scholastic Discovery Boxes: Trees. Scholastic, 1996. This "First Discovery Book" features a look at trees. Children will learn about trees through this reference volume.

Drummer Hoff

Illustrated by Ed Emberley
Written by Barbara Emberley

Prentice-Hall, 1967 • Caldecott Medal, 1968

Introduction

This unique book features a military group who all have a duty to perform. The rhyming text is fun and everyone enjoys the line "Drummer Hoff fired it off!"

Assignment

The rhymes in *Drummer Hoff* are like musical sounds. In this activity, you will learn about music and musical instruments.

Internet Resources

Charlie Horse's Musical Matching Game
   http://www.pbs.org/charliehorse/kids/games/matching/index.html *Activity 1*

The Musicians of Bremen
   http://www.pbs.org/charliehorse/kids/games/bremen/index.html *Activities 2 & 3*

Sing-a-Long Sing Song
   http://www.barneyonline.com/html/music/music.asp (Needs Real Player) *Activity 4*

Karaoke
   http://www.pbs.org/kids/fungames/karaoke/pbssongs.htm *Activity 5*

Activities

1. Click on the squares at the Charlie Horse Musical Magic Pizza Game, using the "Easy" button. How many musical instruments can you find?

2. Fill in the blanks for the Charlie Horse story and click the button to make your own story.

3. Read the story or have your teacher or librarian read it to the group. Was your

story funny, exciting or silly? Did you like your story? Try the story again, using different words.

4. Sing a son with Barney and Friends. Have fun!

5. Karaoke is fun to do and all you need is a Real Audio Player. Click your favorite song and sing along!

Fun Things to Do

There are many types of musical instruments. The following Web page has instructions for making your own Maraca:

http://www.pbs.org/charliehorse/kids/crafts/shaker/index.htm

Get help from your teacher, librarian or parent and make your own band. Using materials from home, what other instruments can you make?

Conclusion

Music is an important part of our lives. Not only is it a creative outlet, music can teach and help children remember and learn.

Educator Notes

Music can be expressed in a variety of ways. Songs are sung and instruments are played. The following books and Internet sites can help extend a study of music and all it offers children.

Children's Music Web

http://www.childrensmusic.org

This is a nice site dedicated to music for children. There are numerous links of educational value, including a list of children's music sites on the web, a music magazine of fun activities and a concert calendar of children's musical events in the United States and throughout the world. The Children's Music Web is a nonprofit group of individuals and corporations involved in music for children.

The Children's Music Web Guide

http://cmw.cowboy.net/WebG/

The Children's Music Web Guide attempts to list every website related to children's music. It does not review or evaluate the links, merely provides links to information on the World Wide Web. Of special interest to educators is the Music Education link and Online Fun for Kids and Families.

Composer of the Month: Vivaldi

http://cnet.unb.ca/achn/kodaly/koteach/resources/compmonviv.html

Each month, a music composer is highlighted with suggested activities, information, pictures and questions of interest. Also included is a link for past Composer of the Month Web pages.

Enjoy Some Magic

http://www.suite101.com/article.cfm/music_education/1520

This article presents characters from the opera *The Magic Flute* and information on Mozart. Educational activities, such as a listening lesson and historical happenings during Mozart's time, can be used in the classroom or library learning environment.

Families of Instruments

http://www.coreknowledge.org/CKproto2/resrcs/lessons/2FamiliesofInstruments.htm

In this lesson plan, children learn to recognize instruments in a orchestra. The lesson plan also provides suggestions for incorporating movement, listening and singing into the study of instrumentation. This website is part of the Core Knowledge™ Foundation founded by E.D. Hirsh, Jr., a professor at the University of Virginia.

Music: The Experience of a Lifetime

http://www.coreknowledge.org/CKproto2/resrcs/lessons/198MusicExp.htm

This is a lesson plan designed for use in a first grade classroom. The unit provides concept objectives, background information, resources, and daily experiences. Skills stressed in this unit are designed to be practiced over time.

Music on Parade: Carnival of Animals

http://www.coreknowledge.org/CKproto2/resrcs/lessons/K98MusicParade.htm

Another Coreknowledge page which includes lesson plans, information and activities suitable for young children. This lesson combines animals and music for a combination of fun and enjoyment.

The Piano Education Page—Just for Kids

http://www.unm.edu/~loritaf/pnokids.html

Contains links developed for children, including Meet the Composer, Having Fun with Piano Lessons, Ask the Teacher and Cool Places for kids. Designed for piano students and those interested in music, information from this page will be useful to supplement a study of music, as it presents a variety of musical activities and information.

The Piano Education Page—Meet the Composer

http://www.unm.edu/~loritaf/pnoschub.html

Franz Schubert is highlighted at this Internet site. Presented in a question and answer format, this site is useful, as it can be adapted for use with the youngest children to provide information on this important composer.

Virtual Music Classroom

http://cnet.unb.ca/achn/kodaly/koteach/resources/toc.html

This is a nice site for educators, librarians and teachers with links for children and educators. Children will enjoy songs and games, while educators will find useful lesson plans, and teaching strategies.

Writing Song Lyrics

http://www.pbs.org/kids/fungames/karaoke/howwr.htm

This site provides information on how to write a song, using the right words and lyrics for the song and how to put words and music together. For children interested in song writing or learning how a song is written, this site will provide useful information.

Books

Cavalier, Debbie, ed. **Lamb Chop's Play-Along.** Warner, 1996. Lamb Chop has long been a favorite of children and adults. In this book, Lamb Chop presents musical history for the younger set.

Danes, Emma. **Music Theory for Beginners.** E D C Publishing, 1997. Young children are introduced to musical theory, history and criticism. Also included are basic techniques of music and music theory. Using pieces of familiar music, children are shown how music is put together and written down.

Dillon, Christine J. **Music**. Hewitt Research Foundation, 1997. This second edition provides musical history and criticism for children in grades 1–3. The information here would nicely supplement a unit on music, as it presents background information suitable for classroom use.

Music. World Book, 1997. Developed by the publisher of *World Book Encyclopedia*, this book is a look at music history and criticism. Though designed for use with children grades three and above, this book contains information which can be adapted for use with children in the primary grades.

Stanley, Leotha A. **Spread My Wings: A Message in the Music.** Musical-Lee Yours, 1996. Another book on musical history and criticism, this book would benefit children ages five to fourteen. The wide age level represents useful material and information for use in a classroom or library setting.

Officer Buckle and Gloria

Peggy Rathmann

Putnam, 1995 • Caldecott Medal, 1996

Introduction

Gloria the Dog is the true star of Officer Buckle's visits to school children. As Gloria is doing her flips and jumps, Officer Buckle delivers safety tips to children. This entertaining book teaches important safety tips.

Assignment

It is very important to be safe in all parts of our lives. Through these activities, you will learn how to be safe, when to be safe, and why to be safe.

Internet Resources

Pool Safety Poster

http://www.greenweb.com.au/freddo/html/pool_safety_poster.html *Activity 1*

Helmet Junction

http://www.nhtsa.dot.gov/kids/biketour/helmet/index.html *Activity 2*

Make a Safety Promise

http://www.ottoclub.org/otto/regular/village/promise/index.html *Activity 3*

Safety Bear Coloring Book

http://www.rcmp-ccaps.com/s-bear.htm *Activity 4*

Street Safety

http://www.parentsclub.com/games/street.html *Activity 5*

Activities

1. Complete the safety quiz, using the words provided. How well did you do? Do you know your pool safety tips?

2. What is the first myth of a bicycle helmet? What is a bicycle helmet designed to do?

3. Make a Safety Promise by choosing one of the animal characters. What promise did you make?

4. Choose a safety poster to print and color. Share your page with your class and explain the safety tip on the poster.

5. What is the main rule of walking? What do you do when you get near the street? Where do you "go?"

Fun Things to Do

Use the Internet address, http://www.sass.ca/kmenu.htm. Select Booklet from the list at the bottom of the screen. Fill in the blanks and continue through the safety tips given by the Alert Twins, and remember to Stay Alert … Stay Safe.

Conclusion

There are many rules which we can follow to stay safe. Through this Internet activity, we have learned some safety rules and met safe people and animals.

Educator Notes

The following is a representative list of Internet sites and literature with a theme of safety. To find Internet sites on child safety on the World Wide Web, please see the Introduction to this volume.

Bike Safety

http://www.ou.edu/oupd/bikesafe.htm

Although designed for students on an university campus, the information presented at this site can be adapted and used with younger children. Good tips for safe bicycle riding are offered, along with tips for riding.

Kid Safety on the Internet

http://www.ou.edu/oupd/kidsafe/start.htm

Children's safety on the Internet is addressed in a one-page summary of tips for safe Net use. Adults who are concerned with this issue may find this information helpful. This page is presented by the University of Oklahoma Department of Public Safety.

Prevent Accidents

http://www.parentsclub.com/games/prevent.html

Another coloring page, this one stresses bicycle safety. The picture shows a child wearing a helmet as she travels on her bicycle. Included are reasons children should wear a safety helmet when bicycle riding.

Safety Bear's Coloring Instructions

http://www.dps.state.ak.us/AST/safety/instruct.htm

This site has numerous coloring pages which can be printed and used with a variety of age groups. Included are safety tips for bicycles, boats, automobiles, 911, and smoke detectors. The pages are nice and children also have an opportunity to write a story about the picture and mail it to Safety Bear.

Safety City

http://www.nhtsa.dot.gov/kids

Hosted by "Vince" and "Larry," the crash test dummies, this page features a safety school, bicycle tour and art gallery. Valuable information on safety of use to both adults and children can be found via the links on this Internet site.

Safety School: Teacher's Lounge

http://www.nhtsa.dot.gov/kids/safeschool/teachers/index.html

The National Highway Highway Transportation Administration has created these pages with lesson plans, coloring books, games for teachers. The information is useful and has child-appeal. This site is part of the site hosted by "Vince" and "Larry," the crash test dummies from television commercials.

Stay Alert... Stay Safe Games

http://www.sass.ca/school99/menu.htm

Lots of familiar games and activities with a safety theme, including word scramble, story writing, bus trip game and coloring pages. Children of all ages can enjoy the activities. Teachers and librarians will be able to incorporate much into learning situations.

Stay Alert... Stay Safe Memory Game

http://www.sass.ca/school99/memory/mschool.htm

Children can play this memory game to test their ability and at the same time learn about safety. Younger children will also be exposed to an Internet site that will give them practice at using a mouse.

Stay Alert... Stay Safe Word Scramble

http://www.sass.ca/school99/scramble/schoolsc.htm

Children will enjoy this game which is played by unscrambling words. At the same time, they are provided answers to safety questions presented on each page. A good site which entertains as it teaches.

Take a Bike

http://family.go.com/Categories/Activities/Features/family_1997_05/famf/famf57rules/famf57rules.html

This Internet site presents games and activities for young children to ensure safety when riding a bicycle. There are also some bicycle games included as a link to this page.

Welcome to the Otto Club

http://www.ottoclub.org

The Otto Club has a lot of fun activities which teach safety to young children. There is a special section for adults called Especially for Grown-Ups with pertinent information and ideas of educational value. Access this part of the site from a banner at the bottom of the second page of the website. Sponsored by AAA.

Make a Safety Card

http://www.ottoclub.org/otto/regular/store/safety-valentine/index.html

A Shockwave plug-in is needed to play this game. For those who do not have Shockwave loaded on their computer, a link is provided.

Books

Levete, Sarah. ***Looking After Myself.*** Millbrook Press, 1998. Children in grades 1–3 can learn safety education and life skills through the use of this book. Adaptable for classroom or library use, this book contains important information for young children.

Mora, Veronica. ***Police Office Safety Tips Activity & Coloring Book.*** Student Lifeline, 1997. This is a 36-page coloring and activity book which offers information on safety issues for children's. The pages in the book are good for teaching safety lessons and help children remember the rules necessary for a safe existence.

Riehecky, Janet. ***The Child's World of Carefulness***. Child's World, 1997. Accidents and safety are stressed in this book designed for children in preschool through second grade. Part of the A Child's World of Values Series.

Springer, Denise. ***Safety for Kids—How to Prepare, Not Scare: Teaching Young Persons Safe Life Skills***. Rhache, 1998. Designed for the youngest child, this book teaches how to be safe and how not to scare children in the process. Safety education is stressed in this book, which can be used in large group settings or one-on-one.

LQ8

Make Way for Ducklings

Robert McCloskey

Viking, 1941 • Caldecott Medal, 1942

Introduction

Mrs. Mallard has decided to take her young ducklings on a walk to their new home. To get home in the Public Garden, Mrs. Mallard and her ducklings must walk through the busy streets of Boston.

Assignment

During this assignment, you will learn about ducks, listen to some duck calls and play some games helping lost ducks.

Internet Resources

Duck Hunt

  http://aurora.york.ac.uk/ducks.html   *Activity 1*

Make Way for Ducklings

  http://www.schon.com/ducklings.html   *Activity 2*

Kids — Learn about Mallard Ducks

  http://www.tpwd.state.tx.us/adv/kidspage/animals/mallard.htm   *Activities 3 & 4*

Ducks Unlimited de Mexico

  http://mercado.infosel.com/dumac/alasv/activida.htm   *Activity 5*

Activities

1. Can you find the duck in Duck Hide No. 2?

2. Where is the sculpture that shows the ducks from *Make Way for Ducklings*?

3. What is another name for the mallard duck?

4. How many eggs does a mother mallard duck lay in her nest?

5. Help Mr. Duck find his way home.

   Bonus: This site has some words written in a foreign language. What is that language?

Fun Things to Do

Print out the map from the following Internet site. Can you draw Mrs. Mallard and her ducklings as they travel to their new home?

   http://www.mcps.k12.md.us/curriculum/socialstd/grade1/Ducklings1.jpg

Conclusion

Sometimes moving to a new home can be scary. Mrs. Mallard and her ducklings had an adventure to remember! Do you have any adventures to remember about moving to a new home or new classroom?

Educator Notes

The following Internet sites and books contain information about ducks and their habitat which can be used in a variety of ways.

The City Naturalist — Mallard Duck

   http://www.nysite.com/nature/fauna/mallard.htm

   Just like Mr. and Mrs. Mallard and their children, these ducks live in a large city—New York City! Here you'll find the origin of the word "mallard," other names by which the mallard duck is known and a description of ducks. Additionally, the reader is provided information on where mallards live in New York City.

Ducks!

   http://www.alaska.net/~cccandc/ducks.htm

   This page was originally published in *The National Homeschool Journal,* and includes good curriculum ideas and activities for use with young children. Lesson One is a unit on *Make Way for Ducklings.*

Ducks Unlimited

   http://www.ducks.org

   Ducks Unlimited was organized to promote and preserve the duck population in North America. This Internet site provides information on this organization.

Make Way for Ducklings

   http://www.mcps.k12.md.us/curriculum/socialstd/grade1/Make_Way.html

   Make Way for Ducklings is the basis for geography and economics lessons suitable for primary-aged children. Included are materials needed, outcomes and indicators and objectives. This site is sponsored by an elementary school in Maryland.

Mallard

http://home.att.net/~DanCowell/mallard.html

This site presents scientific information on the mallard duck. Some of the information can be adapted for use with young children, with some of the scientific facts more suitable for older children. With care and knowledge of the intended audience, teachers and librarians should be able to use this site to extend an unit on ducks.

Mallard Image Gallery

http://www.geocities.com/~lophura/gbwfgallery/mallard2.html

This is a nice site that offers photographs of the mallard duck. The pictures can be viewed in a larger mode by clicking on them with the mouse.

Nebraska Wildlife Sounds

http://ngp.ngpc.state.ne.us/sounds/sounds.html

Listen to the quack of the mallard and view a picture. It is necessary to have the proper sound hardware and software on the computer to listen to the "quack."

Puddler

http://puddler.ducks.org/puddler/

An official site of Ducks Unlimited, this group of Web pages is designed for children. Activities include stories, art work, coloring pages and puzzles.

Quack, Quack: The Ducks Have Hatched

http://www.coreknowledge.org/CKproto2/resrcs/lessons/298Quack.htm

Nine lessons using the theme "ducks," as written for children in first and second grades are presented. Included in the introduction are learning objectives for language arts, math and science. Each specific lesson provides objectives or goals, materials, vocabulary, procedures and evaluation.

TeacherView: Make Way for Ducklings

http://www.eduplace.com/hmco/school/tview/tviews/levine42.html

A teacher-created activity is presented using themes from *Make Way for Ducklings*. This Internet site is sponsored by Houghton Mifflin.

Books

Brenner, Barbara, and Julia Takaya. ***Chibi: A True Story from Japan.*** Houghton Mifflin, 1996. Children grades PK–4 will enjoy this true story, which originated in Japan. In addition to learning about ducks, children will be exposed to the social life and customs of those who live in Japan.

Duckling. Illustrated by Lorella Rizzatti. Random House Books for Young Readers, 1995. This book is a board book, designed for the younger child. The story of the duckling is a nice story, which would benefit a classroom or library setting. This book can be read independently by younger children or is suitable for use with a small group of children in a storytime session.

Loomis, Jennifer. ***A Duck in a Tree.*** Stemmer House, 1997. This simple photo-essay follows a pair of wood ducks through a full migration pattern. The full-color photographs show clear views of the ducks in their habitat while the text explains what's happening.

Freschet, Berniece. **Wood Duck Baby.** Putnam, 1983. Baby ducks are cute, cuddly and yellow. Young children, grades 1–3, will be able to identify with the activities and antics of baby ducks.

McDonald, Mary A. **Ducks.** Child's World, 1997. This Naturebooks Series book features a look at ducks for young children grades 1–6. The information contained would nicely supplement an unit on the study of ducks and their habitat.

Paterson, Katherine. **The Tale of the Mandarin Ducks**. Puffin, 1995. This Japanese folktale, illustrated by Caldecott Medalists, Leo Dillon and Diane Dillon, and retold by Newbery Medal author Katherine Paterson beautifully presents the a story of a devoted pair of mandarin ducks. Children ages five to eight will enjoy the illustrations and fine tale.

Savage, Stephen. **Duck**. Thomson, 1995. A basic introduction to the mallard's life cycle with nice large-scale illustrations. Information includes physical characteristics, nesting, hatching, and diet.

The Girl Who Loved Wild Horses

Paul Goble

Bradbury, 1978 • Caldecott Medal, 1979

Introduction

A Plains Indian girl has a strong friendship with the horses that she lives with. Soon she becomes a horse herself. This is a nice tale drawn from Native American tradition.

Assignment

During this activity, you will learn about horses, see some pictures of horses, and have fun coloring and playing games about horses.

Internet Resources

Jump Puzzle
   http://horsefun.com/puzzles/jumpuz.html   *Activity 1*

Which Two Horses are the Same?
   http://horsefun.com/puzzles/which2.html   *Activity 2*

Coloring
   http://coloring.com/demo/begin.html?img=horsie   *Activity 3*

Pony Ride Puzzle
   http://www.horse-country.com/youngentry/yemarjorie.html   *Activity 4*

Bonnie's Arabian Mare
   http://www.horse-country.com/youngentry/yebamarefoal.html   *Activity 5*

Activities

1. Print out the puzzle and complete the Jump Puzzle. Type your answer in the space provided. Were you correct?

2. What are names of the two horses which are the same?

3. Choose your colors and color the jumping horse. Print your finished project.

4. Print the page and connect the dots. What did you make?

5. Cut out the horses and color. Write a short story or poem about what you see. What are the names of the horses? Where are they going? What is their favorite food?

Fun Things to Do

Print the page located at the following Internet address:

Ramsey's Horse Puzzle

http://www.horse-country.com/youngentry/yeramsey.html

Cut along the black lines and mix up the puzzle pieces. Can you put the puzzle together correctly?

Conclusion

Horses are large animals that do work for the farmer, run on the prairie, and allow people to ride on their backs. Horses are also fun to play games with, like we did today!

Educator Notes

World Wide Web resources and literature specifically for children on the subject of horses include the following sites.

Horse-Country.Com

http://www.horse-country.com/

The home page of an Internet site devoted to children and horses. Included are links for many of the activities in this LearningQuest, a "cyberbarn," and "Young Riders Journal." In addition, there are links for horse history, horse racing, and other Web resources with a horse theme.

Breeds of Horses Word Search

http://www.horse-country.com/youngentry/yebreed.html

Print the page and find the horse words hidden. The words in this activity would make good vocabulary words for use with older children. In addition, there are links for numerous horse breeds presented by Oklahoma State University.

Clara's Card Match

http://www.horse-country.com/youngentry/yeclarecards.html

To play this game, print out the Internet page and cut along solid black lines. Children can practice visual skills by matching pairs of pictures about horses. Use this game for individual skill building or to enlarge and use with a group.

Clara's Matching Objects

http://www.horse-country.com/youngentry/yeclarematch.html

Children are asked to match various horse body parts with the correct answer. It may be necessary to review this subject with children, as not all children will know a "cannon" corresponds with a bone in a horse's leg.

Clara's Pony Feed

http://www.horse-country.com/youngentry/yeclarepony.html

Print the page and follow the trail to give each horse its correct bowl of food. Children will practice visual skills and can have fun at the same time. Extensions to the project could be a discussion of the diet of a horse and proper care.

Connect the Dots

http://www.horse-country.com/youngentry/yedots.html

Print the page and connect the dots. Children will have a finished product of a horse and her foal. This page would make a good project for younger children to practice coloring skills, or as a story starter with older children.

Lucky and Loser

http://horsefun.com/puzzles/luklosr.html

Which pony has an owner who takes good care of it? Children are provided visual clues to the health and environment of two horses and asked to name one "Lucky" and one "Loser." There is also a section that provides the answers and explains why Lucky is lucky and Loser is a loser.

Mr. Ned's Question

http://www.equiworld.net/global/faqs/genquiz/index.htm

This is part of a quiz site at EquiWorld.Net. The quiz is short and simple enough for the youngest child to complete. There are other links included in the pages at http://www.equiworld.net

Ponies

http://www.mda.state.mi.us/kids/countyfair/animals/ponies/index.html

This site is designed for children who like horses and ponies. There are links on pony care, uses for ponies, mothers and foals and a glossary of terminology. This site would be a good source for additional information about horses or a place for children interested in the subject to view.

What Colour Is That?

http://horsefun.com/puzzles/colour.html

Identification of horses by color and markings is featured at this Internet site. Children are asked to correctly match the names to the color description. The answers are provided, as are links to additional puzzles on horses.

Books

Cox, Rhonda. **At the Horse Show**. Richard C. Owen, 1997. Children through the second grade will learn how a real horse show is conducted in this book.

Harris, Richard. ***I Can Read About Horses.*** Troll, 1997. Horses and nature are highlighted in this book intended for grades 2–4. The factual information would benefit a curriculum unit or library program for children with a theme of horses.

Hartley, Linda. ***The Foal Seasons***. Garrett Educational, 1996. Part of the Shining Nature Series, baby horses, or foals, are featured in this book intended for the youngest child through grade 3.

McDonald, Mary A. ***Horses.*** Child's World, 1997. Horses are presented in this installment of The Child's World Nature Books Series. Intended for children grades 2–6, the information presented can be adapted for use with a younger audience.

Paint Works: Horses and Ponies. Advanced Marketing Service, 1996. While intended for use with children on a 3rd grade reading level, *Paint Works: Horses and Ponies*, could be used with younger children.

The Snowy Day

Ezra Jack Keats

Viking, 1962 • Caldecott Medal, 1963

Introduction

Peter has an exciting day as he plays in the snow making tracks and snow angels. He experiments with building a snowman, and even tries to save a snowball in his pocket.

Assignment

Snow is wet, white and very cold. Through the Internet activities listed below, you will have some fun with snow and learn some snow facts as you go. Have a great time, and don't forget to wear your snow boots!

Internet Resources

Winter Wonderland Puzzle

> http://www.themeunits.com/Freebies.html
> Select "Brrr It's Cold! Crossword Puzzle Sample" and download the
> .pdf activity page. *Activity 1*

Let It Snow

> http://familyeducation.com/quiz/0,1399,1-4541,00.html *Activities 2 & 3*

Make a Snowflake

> http://www.muohio.edu/dragonfly/snow/icensnow.HTMLX *Activities 4 & 5*

Activities

1. Print the crossword puzzle and complete, using the picture clues and word bank.

2. Answer the first and second questions in this quiz.

3. If you enjoy snow, continue with this activity. How well did you do?

4. Pick one area and follow the directions to make a snowflake.

5. Describe your snowflake for your classmates.

Fun Things to Do

Make a Snowthing

http://www.afroam.org/children/fun/snowperson/snowperson.html

Someone has built a snowman, but has forgotten it's hat, arms, eyes and nose. Use your computer mouse to finish the snowman. Print your picture and make up a story about your snowman. Share your story with your class members. Shockwave for Director 5 Plug-in is required for this game.

Conclusion

Just like Peter did in *The Snowy Day*, we have had a fun time playing in the snow. And like Peter, we discovered different things about snow and had a busy day. If you've ever tried to save a snowball in your pocket, let everyone know what happened!

Educator Notes

Ezra Jack Keats

http://www.lib.usm.edu/~degrum/EJKeats.htm

The deGrummond Collection at the University of Southern Mississippi is the only repository for the Ezra Jack Keats Archive. A variety of holdings are part of the Keats Archive, including manuscripts, sketches, illustrations and proofs. Included on the page is information on the published works of Ezra Jack Keats and a bibliography of his work.

Kids Snow Page

http://www.teelfamily.com/activities/snow

The Teel Family lives in Alaska and has a very nice Web page with a lot of snow activities. Designed for children, the pages feature information, science activities and other snow links. The site is educational and entertaining, and is a good resource for educational activities.

Snow Activities

http://www.teelfamily.com/activities/snow/activities.html

Included in this page from the Teel Family are a snow scavenger hunt, directions on making an ice candle, things to do outside in the snow, and activities for when it is to cold to play outside. The activities included are fun and adaptable for use in an educational setting or library.

Additional pages on the Teel Family site:

Snow Food

http://www.teelfamily.com/activities/snow/food.html

Doesn't a snow slush cone or snow ice cream sound good? Yum, Yum, Yum!

Snow Links

http://www.teelfamily.com/activities/snow/links.html

A great list of snow links that can be found via the World Wide Web, including science experiments, a snowman math unit and how to build an igloo.

Snow Science
http://www.teelfamily.com/activities/snow/science.html

Snow crystals, catching snowflakes and keeping snowflakes are presented on this page. The information about snow crystals and how they are formed would be useful for use in a science class.

The NSW Snow Camera Page
http://www.ski.com.au/info/snowcams/nsw.html

Here is a view of the snow located at various ski resorts in Australia. During the summer, the Web page features file images from the previous season. This page would be interesting to look at on a daily basis to track snowfall and conditions.

Salt Lake 2002
http://www.SLC2002.org/kids/index.html

The XIX Olympic Winter Games in Salt Lake City, Utah, is the sponsor for this site for kids. Included is a coloring sheet of the Salt Lake City Olympics logo, a snowflake.

Snow/Water/Ice
http://www.minnetonka.k12.mn.us/support/science/lessonsk1/snow.html

This lesson plan provides the objectives, materials and procedure desirable for a study of snow. Originally, developed for the University of Wisconsin-Superior Project, Superior Science.

TeacherView: The Snowy Day
http://www.eduplace.com/hmco/school/tview/tviews/bray12.html

A teacher's view of *The Snowy Day* is presented with a review of the book and activity which centers upon *The Snowy Day*. This page is from Houghton Mifflin.

Books

Carlisle, Madelyn W. **Sparkling, Silent Snow.** Forest House, 1996. Part of the Let's Investigate Series, this book is a look at snow. Intended for use with children in grades two and above, this book would be useful in an educational setting.

Cech, John. **First Snow, Magic Snow**. Simon & Schuster, 1992. This story is a folktale from the Soviet Union. Intended for young children, this nicely illustrated story would work well in a classroom or library setting for a read-a-loud story session.

Merk, Ann. **Rain, Snow & Ice.** Rourke, 1994. The weather is presented for primary aged children, particularly snow, rain and ice. This book is a part of the Weather Report Discovery Library series published by Rourke.

Rothman, Cynthia. **I Love Snow**. Newbridge, 1994. This big book is intended for use in a whole-language situation. The themes of snow and nature can also lead to discussion about conservation. Young children will enjoy the story and adults will find it a useful tool for additional resources and curriculum extenders.

Wetterer, Charles M. **The Snow Walker.** Lerner, 1996. A blizzard has hit New York City and there is snow everywhere. An interesting look at a city as the citizens cope with snow and all its hazards and wonders.

Song and Dance Man

Illustrated by Stephen Gammell
Written by Karen Ackerman
Knopf, 1988 • Caldecott Medal, 1989

Introduction

Grandpa is a song and dance man who enjoys visits from his grandchildren. Grandpa also enjoys taking his grandchildren to the attic in his home where he performs a vaudeville routine, to the delight of everyone.

Assignment

Grandpa was a tap dancer and danced for many audiences. There are many types of dance and people of all ages like to dance. Today you will learn about tap dancing, see a special friend as he dances and have some fun.

Internet Resources

Tera's Elmo Page

    http://www.geocities.com/EnchantedForest/Cottage/9125/elmopage.html   *Activity 1*

Elmo Dances

    http://www.geocities.com/SouthBeach/Docks/2140/celmo.gif   *Activity 2*

Dance Through Your Life

    http://www.offjazz.com/vid-tap.htm   *Activity 3*

Macy's Tap-O-Mania

    http://www.tiac.net/users/tpmac/macys/index.htm   *Activity 4*

Activities

1. Besides playing the violin, what is Elmo's hobby?

2. One of Elmo's favorite things to do is tap dance. Use the Internet address provided to see Elmo dance. Can you do Elmo's dance? Try it!

3. Choose three tap dance steps to view. Which one is your favorite? Can you do the tap dance you liked best?

4. What is the world's record for the greatest number of tap dancers?

Fun Things to Do

The Dancing Teddy is a fun place to visit. Click and play along.

> http://www.pbs.org/teletubbies/games/teddy/tdtshock.html

Did you like the Teddy Bear's dance? Practice the dance and then do the dance for your teacher and class. You need to have the Shockwave plug-in for this site.

Conclusion

We have found out that not only Grandpa from the story *The Song and Dance Man* likes to dance, but so does Elmo! Tap dancing is a hobby practiced by adults and children and enjoyed by many.

Educator Notes

The following Internet sites and books provide a look at the world of Tap Dancing. Some of the material is designed for an older audience, but can be adapted for use with younger children.

Arts Education - Dance

> http://www.sasked.gov.sk.ca/docs/artsed/g3arts_ed/dance009.html
>
> A curriculum guide for the study of dance is presented. Includes a teacher checklist for a sequence of lessons, planning the creative dance lesson, and the five steps to a successful educational unit.

Elmo

> http://members.aol.com/TeenQn/cute.html
>
> Another dancing Elmo site, which is fun for children and adults to watch. Children of all ages love Elmo, and Elmo loves to entertain!

Fancy Dancer

> http://www.poetry4kids.com/fancydancer.html
>
> This site features a cute poem about dancing. Included in the poem are the names of a variety of dances which are all done by Elmo (there's that name again!) Fernando Rodrigo McGants.

Get Real! Story Archives

> http://www.wpt.org/getreal!/500/504/tap.htm
>
> Kids meet C.J., a tap dance student, through the Wisconsin Public Television show, Get Real! Includes Quicktime movie and Real Audio of tap steps and sound.

The Sights and Sounds of Tap

http://www.tapdance.org/tap/sounds/sndclips.htm

This Internet site features video and the sounds of tap dancing. The sounds are nicely done, while the video section is actually a list of other Internet pages which feature tap video. The videos and sounds would aid the visual and auditory learners in the classroom.

Terminology Jazz Dance

http://www.offjazz.com/term-jz.htm

Not only are the steps in tap dance varied, so are the words used to describe it. This page presents information on a variety of vocabulary words, including falls, jumps and pirouettes. The information contained could be used as the basis for a lesson on dance.

Books

Baeza, Silvia P. **Music & Dance.** Rourke Publications, 1995. Music and dance from a Latin-American perspective is the focus of *Music & Dance.* Children in grades 2–6 should benefit from the information found in this volume.

Collier-Morales, Roberta. **Dancers.** Putnam, 1996. This book is part of the Costumes for Coloring Series of books and features a look at dancers for children in grades 2 and up.

Cousin, Patricia T. **Dancing**. Arborlake Publishing, 1995. African American dancing experiences are presented in this multicultural look at the art of dance.

Nye, Penny. **I Love to Dance**. Penny Laine Papers, 1997. Dancing is fun, and many children participate in dancing lessons and recitals. *I Love to Dance* is written for all children who love to dance and those who wish to learn about dancing and its many forms.

Packard, Helen. **A Day in the Life of a Dancer.** Rosen Publishing Group, 1997. For many, dancing is a career. For others it is a hobby. This book, intended for use with children ages four to nine, presents the life of a professional dancer.

Mirette on the High Wire

Emily Arnold McCully

Putnam, 1992 • Caldecott Medal, 1993

Introduction

Mirette lives in Paris in the nineteenth century and helps the former high-wire star Bellini loose his fears. At the same time, she achieves her own dream and walks the high wire.

Assignment

Often the high-wire walker can be found in the circus. It is exciting to visit the circus, look high into the sky to watch a person walk on a thin wire. It is also exciting to be a part of the circus with its animals, clowns and performers. Ladies and Gentlemen, let the show begin!

Internet Resources

Ringling Brothers Barnum & Bailey: History & Tradition

http://www.ringling.com/history   *Activities 1 & 2*

Ringling Brothers Barnum & Bailey: Fun! Games!

http://www.ringling.com/fun/arcade/game_clown.html   *Activity 3*

Under the Big Top: Circus Parade Clowns

http://www.circusparade.com/clowns.htm   *Activity 4*

Activities

1. No one really knows when the Ringling Brothers Barnum & Bailey show began. What are three possible dates for the beginning of this circus?

2. What is another name for the Ringling Brothers Barnum & Bailey Circus?

3. With help from an adult, download the clown game to play on your computer. Did you like playing this game? What does your clown look like?

4. What is another name for a circus clown?

Fun Things to Do

It might be fun to send a e-mail postcard to a friend, teacher, librarian, or classmate. Use the following Internet site and enjoy yourself. You may also wish to share any postcards you receive with your classmates and friends.

Ringling Brothers Barnum & Bailey: Fun! Games! Email!

http://www.ringling.com/fun/ptmail

Conclusion

There is a lot to see and do at the circus. Is your favorite the clowns or the animals? Or maybe you like the high-wire act like Mirette! Whatever you like the best, you can be sure to have a great time when you visit the circus.

Educator Notes

There are some entertaining Web pages on the World Wide Web with a circus theme. Interesting sites cover information on the history, people and animals that make their home "Under the Big Top."

Circus Graphics

http://members.theglobe.com/geronimo25/circus1.html

Free, downloadable circus graphics are provided on this page. Many of the graphics are animated. To download, follow the instructions provided. The images at this site, when printed on a color printer, would be useful as decorations or on a bulletin board. For those without a color printer, the images could be printed and colored with markers or paint.

Circus World Museum

http://www.circusworldmuseum.com

Information at this site is presented by the State Historical Society of Wisconsin's Circus World Museum in Baraboo, Wisconsin. Included are educational, historical and museum display information.

Emily Arnold McCully

http://www.bcpl.lib.md.us/kidspage/mccully.html

The Baltimore County Public Library presents this Web page with information on Emily Arnold McCully, author and illustrator of *Mirette on the High Wire*. It includes a biography and list of books by Ms. McCully. Information here would enhance an author unit of study.

The Great Circus Parade

http://www.circusparade.com

Each year there is a grand, old-time circus parade in Milwaukee, Wisconsin. Additional items of interest from this Web page include the following Internet addresses:

Animals

http://www.circusparade.com/animals.htm

This site tells about the many exotic animals featured in the parade.

Circus Music

http://www.circusparade.com/bands.htm

Information about circus music and marching bands at the parade.

The Great Circus Train

http://www.circusparade.com/train.htm

Photographs and history of the Great Circus Train, which runs once a year from Baraboo, Wisconsin, to Milwaukee, Wisconsin, for the Great Circus Parade.

Ringling Brothers Barnum & Bailey Home Page

http://www.ringling.com/home.jtmpl

This is the home page for The Greatest Show on Earth. Links include fun and games, animals, history and tradition of the circus and circus news. Included is a Ringling Fun Fact which provides trivia and historical facts about the Ringling Brothers Barnum & Bailey Circus.

Books

Chwast, Seymour. *The Twelve Circus Rings.* Harcourt Brace, 1993. Not only is the circus a feature in this book, but young children can practice their counting skills also. Circuses have lots of things to count—Rings, animals, clowns, balloons, laughs … .

Circus. Price Stern Sloan, 1996. The circus is the theme of this Doodle Art 25th Anniversary Series of books. Intended for students ages five to seventeen, adults should find enjoyment with this book as well, as it presents nonfiction information on the circus.

Circus Playscene. Little, Brown, 1996. This book is presented by Duplo, a part of the LEGO family of toys. Duplo is for the youngest child, and this book has an intended audience of preschool and up.

Kalman, Bobbie. *Kids Perform Circus Arts*. Crabtree, 1997. Children ages six to eight will enjoy the aerial acrobats and circus acts featured in this book.

Wawrychuk, Carol. *The Circus: Active Learning about the Arts.* Monday Morning Books, 1998. The study and teaching of art with a circus theme is presented for young children. This book would aid with an unit on the circus or for use in the art classroom with the hands-on art projects that are included.

The Glorious Flight Across the Channel with Louis Bleriot

Alice and Martin Provensen

Viking, 1983 • Caldecott Medal, 1984

Introduction

Louis Bleriot was a Frenchman who was interested in building his own airplane. This story is based on his real life experiences in the early 1900s in France.

Assignment

Like Louis Bleriot, many have been interested in flying. In the United States, the Wright Brothers made an historic flight at Kitty Hawk, North Carolina. Many others like to fly and in this assignment, you will learn about airplanes and flying.

Internet Resources

The "Wright" Stuff

    http://www.faa.gov/education/wright/wright.htm *Activity 1*

Air Bear's Coloring Book

    http://www.alaska.faa.gov/flt_std/aved/AirBear/ABcolordir.html
    Select one of the .pdf versions of the coloring book and download. *Activity 2*

History — Flight to Reality

    http://wings.ucdavis.edu/Book/History/beginner/intro-01.html *Activities 3 & 4*

Activities

1. When did the Wright Brothers make their flight at Kitty Hawk, North Carolina?

2. Select a picture to color and print it out on your home, school or library printer. Use your favorite colors or markers to complete the picture and share with your class or group.

3. What is "lift"? What is "thrust"?

4. What is "control"?

Fun Things to Do

Choose a picture from the Spruce Goose Museum at the following Internet address:

http://sprucegoose.org/sprucegoose/museum/kidzkorner/draw.htm

Print the picture using the printer attached to your computer, and complete. Make up a story about your airplane and write it down or tell to your class. Think about the following questions, maybe you can use them in your story. What kind of airplane is it? Who was flying the airplane? Where were they going?

Conclusion

Many people like to fly. We use airplanes to travel and deliver mail or packages. Without people like Louis Bleriot and The Wright Brothers, we would not be able to fly!

Educator Notes

Numerous sites are available on the Internet which consist of information on aviation. A few selected for use with young children are listed below. Others, while designed for an older age group, can be adapted for educational use.

Canadian Museum of Flight

http://www.canadianflight.org

A nice site with information of use to educators, librarians and parents. You'll find information about aviation history, an art gallery and information about the Canadian Museum of Flight.

FAA Aviation Education

http://www.faa.gov/education/resource/kidcornr.htm

This site features a link to download the "Wilbur and Orville Wright Activity Book." Some of the activities include a word seek using aviation terms, an activity in which children draw their own glider and a map maze. (The book is an .exe file.) There are additional activities, some of which listed on the next page under Kid's Corner, which use the FAA's Alaskan Region website as the source.

First Flight

http://firstflight.open.ac.uk

Provides information on the Wright Brothers. This site also includes a flight simulator and movie.

Flights of Inspiration

http://www.fi.edu/flights

Information on the Wrights' first flight is presented. Also included is a nice teacher resource area that includes curriculum extenders from the website and additional links to more resources for teachers.

LearningQuest 13 : The Glorious Flight Across the Channel

How We Made the First Flight

http://aeroweb.brooklyn.cuny.edu/history/wright/toc.html

The words of Orville Wright have been matched with photos from the initial preparations and the first test flight. This site is nice, as it presents a primary resource for information on flight.

Kid's Corner

http://www.alaska.faa.gov/flt_std/aved/kids/kids.htm

The Federal Aviation Association Alaskan Region home page offers some nice websites for use with children. They include activities for children ages five to nine.

Make Your Own Windmill

http://www.alaska.faa.gov/flt_std/aved/kids/pin%20wheel%205-9.html

Children can construct their own windmill to demonstrate air movement. Follow the directions provided and turn the children loose on a windy day.

Maze

http://www.alaska.faa.gov/flt_std/aved/kids/pictpuz.gif

Print out this maze and children can help the lost pilot find his airplane. Children will enjoy this activity and can color the results.

The Piper Cub

http://www.alaska.faa.gov/flt_std/aved/kids/airplane.gif

A coloring picture of a Piper Club airplane. A small amount of information about the Piper Club is provided.

Learn to Fly

http://www.grouper.com/francois/

Children and adults will enjoy a visit to the Cybercockpit, which shows an airplane cockpit with links to all the instruments. Each instrument link provides information on the functions performed by that instrument.

Slider Puzzle

http://quest.arc.nasa.gov/aero/wright/kids/slider/puzzle.html

A "slider puzzle" in which children can manipulate the squares to complete a picture. This puzzle features the historic Wright Brothers.

Wilbur and Orville Wright

http://www.wam.umd.edu/~stwright/WrBr/Wrights.html

This is a biographical account of the Wright Brothers. You'll find links to their work with flight and a link to additional articles prepared by the Wright Brothers describing their invention of the airplane.

Wright Brothers National Memorial

http://www.nps.gov/wrbr

Presented by the U.S. Department of the Interior, this Web page provides historical, pictorial and educational information from the National Memorial in North Carolina..

The Wright Stuff

http://www.pbs.org/wgbh/pages/amex/wright

This page is devoted to the Wright Brothers and their flight at Kitty Hawk. Featured are a Quicktime movie titled "Return to Kitty Hawk," RealAudio interviews, and a bibliography of sources.

Books

Berger, Melvin and Glenda Berger. ***How Do Airplanes Fly?: A Book About Airplanes***. Hambleton-Hill, 1996. Children ages five to nine will enjoy this book on airplanes and flight. This book is part of the Discovery Readers Series intended for young children.

Petty, Kate. ***Some Planes Hover & Other Amazing Facts About Flying Machines.*** Millbrook, 1998. Not all planes fly, some hover or glide. This book explains the variety of flight conducted by airplanes.

Pluckrose, Henry. ***In the Air.*** Children's Press, 1994. Air and flight go together, especially in this book for children preschool through 3rd grade.

Rowe, Julian and Molly Perham. ***Flying High.*** Children's Press, 1994. A book of flight for young children, this book will aid the educator in preparing information for absorption by young learners.

Scholastic Staff. ***Taking Flight: A Book About Flight***. Scholastic, 1997. This book is from The Magic School Bus Series, and presents flight and aviation for young readers. The factual information presented would benefit and entertain children through use of the story and illustrations.

Tuesday

David Wiesner

Clarion Books, 1991• Caldecott Medal, 1992

Introduction

While this book has few words, the pictures are really neat! Frogs flying on lily pads get into all types of situations as they travel on a Tuesday evening. We can't wait until next Tuesday!!

Assignment

While frogs do not fly, they are interesting creatures. In this LearningQuest, you will learn about frogs and look at some silly pictures.

Internet Resources

Weird Frog Facts
> http://allaboutfrogs.org/weird/weird.html *Activity 1*

So Many Frogs!
> http://allaboutfrogs.org/weird/general/many.html *Activity 2*

Froggy Sounds
> http://frog.simplenet.com/froggy/sounds.shtml (Requires sound.) *Activity 3*

The Jumping Frog
> http://allaboutfrogs.org/funstuff/java/frog.html *Activity 4*

Color Me Frog!
> http://allaboutfrogs.org/funstuff/colorme.html *Activity 5*

Activities

1. What is a frog?

2. What is a group of frogs called?

3. Listen to three frog sounds. Can you make those sounds? Practice and share your frog sounds with your classmates. Which frog sound was your favorite? Why?

4. Can you see the jumping frog? Hurry, there he goes ....

5. Choose a picture to color and print using the "print" button on the computer. Color and share with your class members. Don't forget to give your frog a name!

Fun Things to Do

Some people look strange. Especially when they turn into frogs! Click on the image and you can see your entire computer screen "morph" into a frog:

http://allaboutfrogs.org/funstuff/morph.html

Conclusion

Often we find frogs near the water and hear them as they sing their "songs." Now, we have found frogs on computers and they are just as interesting as the ones on the lily pad!

Educator Notes

A lot of people study and enjoy frogs. A few Internet sites have been chosen here for their educational value and ease of use in the classroom.

Animated Froggies

http://allaboutfrogs.org/gallery/animations/index.html

Animated frog images that can be downloaded for classroom, library or home use. These are images only, frogs are not identified and there is no background information.

The Beacon Art Gallery

http://www.omen.net.au/~beacy/art/frogs/Frog.htm

This site presents art projects created by children, using the theme of frogs. A variety of mediums were used, and each project is available to view at close-up range.

Frogs: A Thematic Unit Plan

http://ericir.syr.edu/Virtual/Lessons/Science/Biological/BIO0029.html

This second grade unit is from the AskEric Virtual Lesson Plan site. The plan offers objectives, unit design for various curriculum areas and an introductory lesson plan.

How Long Do Frogs Live?

http://allaboutfrogs.org/weird/general/longevity.html

Brief educational information on the life span of frogs is given. A list of frogs and their average age is available, as is a searchable database.

Move the Desks! The Pond Is Coming!

http://www.imsa.edu/team/spi/impact2/1993/93PAGE46.HTM

A classroom experience in which children learn about the life cycle and habitat of the frog.

Designed for children in grades K–3, this Web page provides the classroom teacher with methodology, materials and resources.

Songs of the Frog

http://frog.simplenet.com/froggy/songs.shtml

Words to several froggy "songs" that are bound to be popular with students. Titles include "Bein' Green," "Frogs at School," Frog Went a Courtin'" and "Spotted Frog."

Teachers Corner

http://allaboutfrogs.org/info/teach/learning.html

The Frogland Internet site has a section devoted to teacher ideas and links to information about frogs to be found on the World Wide Web. The author requests "froggy" classroom ideas for inclusion on this site.

Books

Crewe, Sabrina. **The Frog.** Raintree Steck-Vaughn, 1997. The life cycle of a frog is presented for children. Intended for use with children in grades 2–5, the information presented can be adapted for use with younger children.

Lovette, Sarah. **Extremely Weird Frogs**. Davidson Titles, 1997. Some frogs are "weird" looking to children and adults. This book from the Extremely Weird Series highlights the unusual of the frog species.

Martin, James. **Frogs.** Crown, 1997. This book will work well with first and second grade children who are good readers and interested in the subject of frogs. The factual information contained in the book could be used in a classroom to enhance a science unit.

Milton, Ann. **Ask Me If I Am a Frog.** Stemmer House, 1998. Young children will enjoy this book and may begin asking you if you are a frog.

Patent, Dorothy H. **Flashy Fantastic Rain Forest Frogs**. Walker, 1997. Creatures in the rain forests are colorful, interesting and exotic. This volume presents information on frogs found in the tropical rain forests of the southern hemisphere.

Rapunzel

Paul O. Zelinsky

Dutton, 1997 • Caldecott Medal, 1998

Introduction

Rapunzel is the story of a beautiful girl kept in a tower by an evil witch. By letting down her long, long hair, Rapunzel's friend the Prince can visit.

Assignment

The Caldecott Medal is awarded for pictures in children's books. Rapunzel's illustrations were done by Paul O. Zelinsky. Mr. Zelinsky is very good at art. During this assignment, we will take an art quiz, learn about color, and see some great pictures from other kids.

Internet Resources

KinderArt Quiz

    http://www.kinderart.com/quiz.htm   *Activity 1*

Art Terms

    http://www.kinderart.com/kterms.htm   *Activities 2 & 3*

Tasty Color Mixing

    http://www.bconnex.net/~jarea/across/tasty.htm   *Activity 4*

Activities

1. Take the KinderArt Quiz. How well did you do? What did you learn?

2. Why type of paint is "acrylic"?

3. Click on the letter "H" and find the word "hue." What does this word mean?

4. What are the three main colors that make all other colors? What two colors make orange? What two colors make violet? What two colors mixed together will make green? What are these colors called?

Fun Things to Do

Visit the KinderArt Fridge Door Gallery at:

http://www.bconnex.net/~jarea/fridge.htm

Choose a door and view the pictures. Which picture do you like the best. With parent, teacher or librarian's help, you can e-mail your own picture for the door!

Conclusion

Art is more than colors. It is painting, drawing and creating. Many types of art are done by artists, including those who illustrate Caldecott Medal books.

Educator Notes

The interactive nature of the Internet makes it a natural source for information on art curriculum and extenders. The following sites offer ideas, lessons and activities for young children.

Art Teacher on the Net

http://www.artmuseums.com

Free art ideas for kids, parents and teachers. You'll find a nice selection of activity links for classroom projects, educational sites, art projects of the week, and drawing lessons for children on this award-winning site. Continue scrolling through this long home page to see all the choices provided.

The Art Teacher Connection

http://www.inficad.com/~arted

This website is for art teachers, art students and classroom teachers who wish to incorporate art into curriculum. Included are World Wide Web art lessons, information about the author of the website and links to art information on the web.

ARTSEDGE: Curriculum Studio

http://artsedge.kennedy-center.org/cs.html

Designed for educators, this site from The Kennedy Center for the Arts, provides K–12 educators with curriculum information on the arts.

ARTSEDGE: For Students

http://artsedge.kennedy-center.org/4stu.html

The Kennedy Center for the Arts has a section for children which features student research pages, and links to pages intended for use by children. For Students is intended to be a place for children to participate in interactive arts-based activities.

ArtsEdNet

http://www.artsednet.getty.edu

This site offers lesson plans and curriculum guides, image galleries, discussion, Web links and a search function. Educators, librarians and parents seeking art curriculum help should find information to aid in their curriculum goals.

Ask Prunella

http://www.pbs.org/wgbh/arthur/prunella/cootie/index.html

Children enjoy Cootie Catchers and can ask their own questions of Prunella, Arthur's friend from the PBS kids show. Sample questions could be "Is red my favorite color?" "Will Rapunzel live happily ever after?" Or "Am I a great artist?"

Color-Me Posters

http://www.execpc.com/~byb/paint.html

Choose from "Gary the Goat," "Roberta the Rabbit," or "Sofie the Sheep." Children can print the pictures and color or paint.

Foundations in Art

http://www.coreknowledge.org/CKproto2/resrcs/lessons/kfndsart.htm

The Core Knowledge website features lessons which meet specific educational goals and objectives. This particular lesson is for use in the kindergarten level, but applies to older children as well.

The Incredible Art Department

http://www.artswire.org/kenroar

The world of art is presented through various venues. Included are art news, lessons, cartoons and an art site of the week. Educators wishing background information on a particular subject may find this site or one of its links useful.

Lesson Plans

http://educate.si.edu/resources/lessons/artlist2.html#start

Lessons plans for activities in the arts. This site is part of the Smithsonian Institution educational offerings.

Paul O. Zelinsky: Artist's Notes on the Creation of *Rapunzel*

Http://www.penguinputnam.com/catalog/yreader/authors/2855_note.html

Paul Zelinksy has written his ideas on the creation of his Caldecott Medal book *Rapunzel*. Included is his thoughts on the text and the pictures he created for the book.

Self Portraits

http://www.primenet.com/~arted/pages/artgallery.html

Children in grades 2–4 have drawn and painted their self portraits and now they reside on the Internet. This Web page is presented by an elementary art teacher at the Herrea School for the Fine Arts in Phoenix, AZ.

Books

Chapman, Laura H. **Adventures in Art.** Davis Publications, 1998. This six-volume set features art activities for children in grades 1–6. Also included is a Teacher's Education/Instructors Manual. Each volume is available separately from the publisher.

Cummings, Pat. **Talking With Artists**. Simon & Schuster. 3 vols. Older children, especially aspiring artists, will enjoy these stories of personal journeys by successful children's illustrators. Includes color photos of artists and their works.

dePaola, Tomie. **The Art Lesson.** Putnam, 1997. Tomie dePaola is enjoyed by many children for his stories and pictures. This autobiographical picture book tells of his dream as a young child to be an artist.

Getty J. Paul, Museum Staff. **A Is for Artist: A Getty Museum Alphabet.** J. Paul Getty Trust, 1997. The alphabet is presented in art form, including paintings and drawings. This book is presented by a well-known museum of art.

LaValette, Desiree, and Gerdt Fehrle. **Keith Haring: I Wish I Didn't Have to Sleep.** te Neues, 1997. Keith Haring was an American artist who lived from 1958–1990, when he died of AIDS. This book presents information on Mr. Haring and his art for children in grades 1–3. For additional information, visit www.haringkids.com.

Van Der Meer, Ron, and Frank Whitford. **The Kids' Art Pack**. D K, 1997. Children will enjoy this book which presents juvenile art activities and expression.

Arrow to the Sun

Gerald McDermott

Viking, 1974 • Caldecott Medal, 1975

Introduction

The Lord of the Sun's child travels to find his father and along the way must prove his relationship to the Sun. This story is from a Pueblo Indian legend.

Assignment

Our sun and planets are interesting to explore. During this assignment, you will learn about the sun and some of the planets that make up our solar system.

Internet Resources

Kids Space: How old would you be?
   http://liftoff.msfc.nasa.gov/kids/solarsys/age.html   *Activity 1*

Kids Space: How much would you weigh?
   http://liftoff.msfc.nasa.gov/kids/solarsys/weight.html   *Activity 2*

Kids Coloring Page
   http://liftoff.msfc.nasa.gov/kids/adventure/coloring/Solar_System.html   *Activity 3*

Kids Space: Quiz
   http://liftoff.msfc.nasa.gov/kids/adventure/quiz/quiz1.html   *Activity 4*

Activities

1. How old would you be if you lived on Venus? Jupiter? Pluto?

2. How much would you weigh if you lived on Mars, Saturn? Neptune?

3. Print out the coloring page and color. Which planet is the largest on the page? The smallest?

4. Take the Kid's Space Quiz. How well did you do? Be sure to complete your Award at the end of the quiz.

Fun Things to Do

Scout is lost in space and needs your help. Use the following Internet address to help Scout find something to wear while lost.

http://www.afroam.org/children/fun/scoutspace/scoutspace.html

Note: To play the game, Shockwave for Director 5 must be loaded.

Conclusion

Wouldn't it be exciting to explore the planets in our solar system? Or would you rather stay on Earth? You can always explore the planets by using your computer and the World Wide Web.

Educator Notes

The following Internet sites contain information which can be adapted for use in a lower elementary classroom. Additionally, literature on the solar system suitable for use with children are included in the Educator Notes.

Lost in Space

http://www.coreknowledge.org/CKproto2/resrcs/lessons/198LostSpace.htm

This month long unit on the solar system is designed for first graders. The lessons at this Internet site focus on language arts, mathematics and science.

NASA (National Aeronautics and Space Administration) Home Page

http://www.nasa.gov

The NASA space program has a long history and potential for varied use in educational settings. This Web page offers information on current NASA projects, history of NASA and educational resources. Selected pages of interest are described below.

Additional NASA pages of interest

NASAKIDS

http://kids.msfc.nasa.gov

Especially for children, NASAKIDS offers plenty of activities, games and information on space exploration that can be used in the classroom. There is also a "Teacher's Corner" located at this site.

Lift Off Space Art Gallery

http://kids.msfc.nasa.gov/Gallery/gallery.asp

Visit the art gallery and take a tour of the solar system, as presented by children. This site would be good for use in an art class or to further the study of the solar system. Children will enjoy viewing the work of their peers.

Make a Sundial

http://liftoff.msfc.nasa.gov/kids/Earth/SundialMake.html

With help from an adult, children can construct a sundial. In the process, children can learn about latitude and telling time via the sun. Also, children can learn some history associated with telling time.

Observatorium

http://observe.ivv.nasa.gov/nasa/core.shtml

The Observatorium has a collection of breathtaking and awe-inspiring images of Earth and space. Along with photographs of the Earth, planets, stars, and "other cool stuff," are information stories and background information.

Solar System

http://kids.msfc.nasa.gov/Puzzles/SolarSystem.asp

By placing the planet on the appropriate ring in this game, children are taught the proper order of the planets in our solar system. At the same time, they have fun and can view photographs of each planet.

Welcome to the Planets

http://pds.jpl.nasa.gov/planets

This Internet site features images from NASA's exploration of our solar system. Children can click on a planet and discover factual information about the particular planet. Includes a glossary of terms.

The Planets

http://nyelabs.kcts.org/teach/episodeguides/eg41.html

This Internet site is from an episode presented by Bill Nye. Facts, experiments, and a list of books for further reading are included. The introduction is short and presented so children can understand the information presented.

Solar System Mobile

http://www.geocities.com/Heartland/7134/Fun/crafts1.htm

Complete instructions and graphics are included at this Internet site for constructing a solar system mobile. Adult supervision will be necessary for use with younger children. The finished project would make a nice display when hung from light fixtures.

The Sun

http://nyelabs.kcts.org/teach/episodeguides/eg33.html

The sun is very large, and Bill Nye presents information and further reading about the sun on this episodeguide page. However, to see the interactive parts of this website, plug-ins are needed. MacroMedia Flash is needed to enter the website through the home page. In the full site there is an experiment for students on how sunshine makes energy.

To Infinity and Beyond—Space

http://www.coreknowledge.org/CKproto2/resrcs/lessons/198Infinity.htm

Designed for first graders, To Infinity and Beyond teaches the solar system. An overview, teacher resources, activities, materials and objectives for a variety of learning areas are included.

Books

Becklake, Sue. *Space*. World Book, 1997. This book is a picture reference book which contains information designed for young children. Topics include astronomy, outer space, solar system and astronautics.

Caudle, Brad. *Solar System*. Rock 'n Learn, 1997. This book comes with an audiocassette to enhance the learning process. Children ages seven and up will learn about the solar system as they listen to the accompany cassette.

Cole, Joanna. *Hello Out There*. Scholastic, 1995. Astronomy and the solar system are the focus of this book in the Magic School Bus series. Joanna Cole is known for her factual, informative and entertaining books for young children.

Davis, Amanda. *Our Solar System*. Rosen Publishing Group, 1997. Children through the fourth grade have the opportunity to explore the solar system through the use of this book. The book is part of the Exploring Science Series.

Solar System. Price Stern Solan, 1996. With this book, children of all ages will learn about the solar system and practice their art skills as well.

Abraham Lincoln

Ingri and Edgar Parin d'Aulaire

Doubleday, 1939 • Caldecott Medal, 1940

Introduction

Abraham Lincoln was the sixteenth president of the United States. This book is a picture book biography of Mr. Lincoln's life. You will learn about Mr. Lincoln and the United States in the 1800s.

Assignment

Through the Internet, you will learn about Abraham Lincoln and understand some events that were happening in our country during his presidency.

Internet Resources

Abraham Lincoln Quiz

http://www.siec.k12.in.us/~west/proj/lincoln/quiz.htm   *Activity 1*

Abraham Lincoln

http://www.americanpresidents.org/presidents/president.asp?PresidentNumber=16
Activity 2

Treasure Hunt

http://www.siec.k12.in.us/~west/proj/lincoln/treasure.htm   *Activity 3*

Ask a Question

http://www.siec.k12.in.us/~west/proj/lincoln/ask.htm   *Activity 4*

Activities

1. After reading the 1940 Caldecott Medal Book, *Abraham Lincoln*, take the online quiz about Abraham Lincoln.

2. When was Abraham Lincoln president?

3. Try the treasure hunt to learn more about Abraham Lincoln.

4. If you could ask Abraham Lincoln a question, what would it be? With permission of a parent, teacher or librarian, ask "Mr. Lincoln" a question using the provided Internet address.

Fun Things to Do

With an adult, read the Emancipation Proclamation by using the provided link at the following Internet address:

http://www.thelincolnmuseum.org/education/teachers_guide/imagination.html

How would you feel if you were a slave living in 1862? A slave owner? The President?

Complete the questions at this Internet site and talk about your answers with an adult.

Conclusion

Abraham Lincoln was a famous person in the history of the Untied States. He is remembered for working to free the slaves and save the union of states. Reading about the lives of great people is interesting and allows you to remember those who worked to make the world a better place to live.

Educator notes

The majority of Internet sites on Abraham Lincoln are designed for use with older children and adults. The first few sites in this list are designed for use with young children, while the remaining contain material which can be adapted.

Abraham Lincoln

http://www.triax.com/glxyclbamr/lincoln.htm

This site presents facts and information about Abraham Lincoln. Included is a short speech given by Lincoln and a photograph of the young President of the Untied States.

Abraham Lincoln

http://www.ipl.org/ref/POTUS/alincoln.html

Abraham Lincoln information, including biographies, other Internet resources and references, as presented by The Internet Public Library, (IPL). The IPL is an extensive site with information, activities for children and resources for adults.

Abraham Lincoln

http://www.whitehouse.gov/WH/glimpse/presidents/html/al16.html

This Internet site is presented by The White House in Washington DC. It provides facts, figures, and links to further information about Abraham Lincoln. Also included are quotes from his writings and speeches.

Abraham Lincoln

http://sc94.ameslab.gov/TOUR/alincoln.html

This is a nice site with much information on Lincoln's early years, and work as a legislator, lawyer and President. Included is information on Lincoln's stance on slavery and information on the Civil War. This all-text site has information which can be used with younger children. This page is presented as part of a Washington D.C. sightseeing site recommended by the History Channel.

Classroom Activities

http://www.siec.k12.in.us/~west/proj/lincoln/class.htm

A first grade class developed some of the Internet activities used in this LearningQuest. This site is a listing of classroom activities which incorporate the study of Abraham Lincoln into various curriculum. Included is using a search engine to search for facts about Lincoln, additional resource sites and information on the different sections of the Web page.

From a Log Cabin to the White House

http://www.coreknowledge.org/CKproto2/resrcs/lessons/298LogCabin.htm

This lesson plan for second-grade children incorporates a study of Abraham Lincoln into the elementary curriculum. An extensive list of literature resources is a nice feature of this site.

The History Place Presents Abraham Lincoln

http://www.historyplace.com/lincoln/index.html

This Internet site features a timeline of Lincoln's life; photographs of him, his family and important events of the Civil War; and speeches presented by Lincoln. In addition, there are links to the Emancipation Proclamation, Battle of Gettysburg, Kansas-Nebraska Act, and Dred Scott Decision.

Lincoln Assassination Trial

http://members.aol.com/RVSNorton/Lincoln18.html

In 1865, a trial was held to determine the charge of conspiracy in the death of Abraham Lincoln. This Internet site lists information about that trial and the people who were accused of conspiracy. Also included are links to actual testimony of the trial, photos of the accused conspirators, and in-depth information on John Wilkes Booth.

Lincoln Crossword Puzzle

http://www.thelincolnmuseum.org/education/teachers_guide/crossword.html

Children can print the crossword puzzle and complete using clues from Abraham Lincoln's life and work as 16th President of the United States. Younger children may need assistance from an adult or older child to complete the crossword, but they will gain knowledge by completing this exercise.

Quick Facts: Abraham Lincoln

http://gi.grolier.com/presidents/aae/quickfac/16flinc.html

Grolier Online has a short page which highlights major events in the life of Abraham Lincoln. Included are links for his Inaugural Address and other areas of interest about the sixteenth President of the United States.

Books

Abraham Lincoln. Troll Communications, 1996. A look at the presidency of Abraham Lincoln, this book would be good for use with children ages seven to ten.

LearningQuest 17 : Abraham Lincoln

Barkan, Joanne. **Abraham Lincoln & President's Day: Let's Celebrate.** Silver Burdett Press, 1996. Designed for young children, this book is a study of Abraham Lincoln and his presidency.

MacMillan, Dianne M. **Presidents Day.** Enslow Publishers, 1997. This book features information on George Washington and Abraham Lincoln, for whom we remember during Presidents Day, held each year in February.

Mosher, Kiki. **Learning About Honesty from the Life of Abraham Lincoln.** Rosen Publishing Group, 1996. Abraham Lincoln is known as "Honest Abe," and this book, presented in story format, provides lessons on honesty and truthfulness for young children.

Usel, T. M. **Abraham Lincoln.** Children's Press, 1996. Part of the Read & Discover Biographies Series, this book looks at the life of Abraham Lincoln. Young children ages five through eight will learn about Abraham Lincoln through illustrations, photos and factual information.

Snow Flake Bentley

Illustrated by Mary Azarian
Written by Jacqueline Briggs Martin

Houghton Mifflin, 1998 • Caldecott Medal, 1999

Introduction

From the time he was a small boy Wilson Bentley has been interested in the snow crystals that fall near his home in Vermont. He dreams of using a camera to take pictures of the snow and study each flake. Little did he know that his dream would become an important discovery!

Assignment

Wilson Bentley wanted to take pictures. Often we take pictures to remember a fun event or special time. It is exciting to look at the pictures we have taken. In this LearningQuest, you will learn about the history of photography and have fun while you do.

Internet Resources

Expedition Riverside
> http://www.cmp.ucr.edu/site/exhibitions/exped/ph1.html   *Activity 1*

Dinosaur Hall
> http://photo2.si.edu/dino/dino.html   *Activities 2 & 3*

Scribble Pad
> http://www.cs.reading.ac.uk/people/jpb/children/scribble.html   *Activity 4*

Activities

1. View the photographs contained on this Web page. Write a short story about what is happening.

2. Look at the photographs of the Allosaurus dinosaur. Where was this picture taken? Who took it?

3. Look at the Stegosaurus dinosaur. When did this dinosaur live? Can you guess how many bones a Stegosaurus has?

4. Pretend you are going to photograph a picture you made of your house. Use the scribble pad to draw a picture of your house. Don't forget any trees, the grass or the sun!

Fun Things to Do

Use the following address to see pictures from the collections of the Smithsonian Institution, our national museum:

   http://photo2.si.edu/contents.html

From the list of subjects, pick three Web links that interest you and look at the photographs on those pages. Which pictures were your favorites? Do you think you could take pictures like those you saw? Did you see pictures of people, animals, or objects? Have fun and share your favorite pictures with your class.

Conclusion

Taking pictures is fun. Pictures are a way to record things that happen to us, places we've been and people that are important to us. Sometimes a picture helps us remember an event or activity. Sometimes pictures make us laugh. Whatever the reason, taking pictures is a fun activity and can be something we enjoy for many years.

Educator notes

The American Museum of Photography

   http://www.photographymuseum.com/index.html

   Students can view a variety of photographic exhibitions and learn about the museum and research being done on photography. The exhibits are of nice value, as they present a history of our world as seen through the eyes of its participants.

Desert Light Photos

   http://www.eduhelp.com/desertlight.html

   There are numerous Web pages that feature photographs. This particular page features photos of the southwestern United States as seen through the camera of an art teacher. Children and adults alike will enjoy this site, that can be used as an appreciation for beauty, study of photography, or geography lessons.

George Eastman

   http://www.kbnet.co.uk/rleggat/photo/history/eastman.htm

   Provides a short biographical introduction to George Eastman, who is considered to be the person that made photography available to the masses. This site would be a good starting point for a study of the history of photography.

Kodak: How to make and Use a Pinhole Camera

http://www.kodak.com/global/en/consumer/education/lessonPlans/pinholeCamera/index.shtml

A classroom activity in which students and instructor make and use a pinhole camera. A description of a pinhole camera is provided, as are directions for making a pinhole camera. This activity would be a fun introduction to the wonders of photography.

Kodak: Know Your Town: Let Your Town Know You!

http://www.kodak.com/global/en/consumer/education/lessonPlans/lessonPlan146.shtml

Describes an activity completed by an elementary school in which they photographed various aspects of their town. Included is a good narrative, materials list and evaluation. Of special note is the list of activities that can be included in a photographic essay.

Kodak: Our School

http://www.kodak.com/global/en/consumer/education/lessonPlans/lessonPlan052.shtml

This lesson plan is designed for young children as an introduction to art photography and creative writing. Children decided on topics to be included and learned to operate a simple 35 mm camera. This plan provides the educator with a purpose and description, activities, materials and outcomes.

Photo Interactive

http://library.advanced.org/11355/html/edindex2.htm

The Photo Interactive website contains the two pages below, plus a host of other sites useful in education. Of special interest will be the interactive camera quiz found under section number 1, and information on taking a picture. Other sites at the Photo Interactive Web page are:

Parts of a Camera

http://library.advanced.org/11355/html/partsofcamera.htm

There is more to the camera than meets the eye. This website will provide all ages with information on the camera and how it is used to take pictures. Readers can learn the parts of a camera and their functions, types of cameras and view photographs.

Types of Cameras

http://library.advanced.org/11355/html/types.htm

A this part of the site, linked to the Parts of Camera Web page listed above, learners will be exposed to a variety of camera types used in photography.

Pretty, Perfect Pet Pictures

http://www.apogeephoto.com/mag3-6/mag3-6pet.shtml

This Web page provides information for children on photographing pets. While some of the information may be too advanced for younger children, an educator can adapt and use the activity to enhance a learning situation. Some of the terminology would be good for children, as they will gain exposure to the "words" of pictures.

Books

Gentieu, Penny. ***Wow! Babies.*** Crown Books for Young Readers, 1997. Everyone enjoys looking at their baby pictures, and this book will provide a good discussion of babies, how people change and photography.

Geddes, Anne. ***My First Five Years***. CEDCO, 1997. Anne Geddes is famous for her inventive photographs of children. This book will appeal to children and adults and is only one of her many works available via literature, cards and calendars.

Joseph, Paul. ***George Eastman.*** Abdo and Daughters, 1996. This book is a biography of George Eastman and features good background information about his life, cameras and photography.

Gibbons, Gail. ***Click! A Book About Cameras and Taking Pictures.*** Little, Brown, 1997. A good introduction to taking pictures, this book would be suitable for classroom, home and library use. Gail Gibbons is known for her scientific books on a variety of subjects such as nature, holidays, and astronomy.

Wick, Walter. ***Walter Wick's Optical Tricks.*** Scholastic, 1998. A good classroom challenge for the visually perceptive. These photographic illusions of inanimate objects will give students some new perspectives on what can be accomplished with the camera. A real art experience.

Caldecott Medal Books

1999	***Snowflake Bentley*** (Houghton Mifflin)	Illustrated by Mary Azarian Written by Jacqueline Briggs Martin
1998	***Rapunzel*** (Dutton)	Paul O. Zelinsky
1997	***Golem*** (Clarion)	David Wisniewski
1996	***Officer Buckle and Gloria*** (Putnam)	Peggy Rathmann
1995	***Smoky Night*** (Harcourt)	Illustrated by David Diaz Written by Eve Bunting
1994	***Grandfather's Journey*** (Houghton)	Allen Say
1993	***Mirette on the High Wire*** (Putnam)	Emily Arnold McCully
1992	***Tuesday*** (Clarion Books)	David Wiesner
1991	***Black and White*** (Houghton)	David Macaulay
1990	***Lon Po Po: A Red-Riding Hood Story from China*** (Philomel)	Ed Young
1989	***Song and Dance Man*** (Knopf)	Illustrated by Stephen Gammell Written by Karen Ackerman
1988	***Owl Moon*** (Philomel)	Illustrated by John Schoenherr Written by Jane Yolen
1987	***Hey, Al*** (Farrar)	Illustrated by Richard Egielski Written by Arthur Yorinks
1986	***The Polar Express*** (Houghton)	Chris Van Allsburg
1985	***Saint George and the Dragon*** (Little, Brown)	Illustrated by Trina Schart Hyman Written by Margaret Hodges

1984	***The Glorious Flight: Across the Channel with Louis Bleriot*** (Viking)	Alice & Martin Provensen
1983	***Shadow*** (Scribner)	Marcia Brown
1982	***Jumanji*** (Houghton)	Chris Van Allsburg
1981	***Fables*** (Harper)	Arnold Lobel
1981	***Ox-Cart Man*** (Viking)	Illustrated by Barbara Cooney Written by Donald Hall
1979	***The Girl Who Loved Wild Horses*** (Bradbury)	Paul Goble
1978	***Noah's Ark*** (Doubleday)	Peter Spier
1977	***Ashanti to Zulu: African Traditions*** (Dial)	Illustrated by Leo & Diane Dillon Written by Margaret Musgrove
1976	***Why Mosquitoes Buzz in People's Ears: A West African Tale*** (Dial)	Illustrated by Leo & Diane Dillon Retold by Verna Aardema
1975	***Arrow to the Sun*** (Viking)	Gerald McDermott
1974	***Duffy and the Devil*** (Farrar)	Illustrated by Margot Zemach Retold by Harve Zemach
1973	***The Funny Little Woman*** (Dutton)	Illustrated by Blair Lent Written by Arlene Mosel
1972	***One Fine Day*** (Macmillan)	Nonny Hogrogian
1971	***A Story, A Story: An African Tale*** (Atheneum)	Gail E. Haley
1970	***Sylvester and the Magic Pebble*** (Windmill Books)	William Steig
1969	***The Fool of the World and the Flying Ship*** (Farrar)	Illustrated by Uri Shulevitz Written by Arthur Ransome
1968	***Drummer Hoff*** (Prentice-Hall)	Illustrated by Ed Emberley Written by Barbara Emberley
1967	***Sam, Bangs & Moonshine*** (Holt)	Evaline Ness
1966	***Always Room for One More*** (Holt)	Illustrated by Nonny Hogrogian Written by Sorche Nic Leodhas
1965	***May I Bring a Friend?*** (Atheneum)	Illustrated by Beni Montresor Written by Beatrice Schenk de Regniers
1964	***Where the Wild Things Are*** (Harper)	Maurice Sendak
1963	***The Snowy Day*** (Viking)	Ezra Jack Keats
1962	***Once a Mouse*** (Scribner)	Marcia Brown

1961	**Baboushka and the Three Kings** (Parnassus)	Illustrated by Nicolas Sidjakov Written by Ruth Robbins
1960	**Nine Days to Christmas** (Viking)	Marie Hall Ets Written by Aurora Labastida
1959	**Chanticleer and the Fox** (Crowell)	Barbara Cooney
1958	**Time of Wonder** (Viking)	Robert McCloskey
1957	**A Tree Is Nice** (Harper)	Illustrated by Marc Simont Written by Janice Udry
1956	**Frog Went a Courtin'** (Harcourt)	Illustrated by Feodor Rojankovsky Written by John Langstaff
1955	**Cinderella, or the Little Glass Slipper** (Scribner)	Marcia Brown
1954	**Madeline's Rescue** (Viking)	Ludwig Bemelmans
1953	**The Biggest Bear** (Houghton)	Lynd Ward
1952	**Finders Keepers** (Harcourt)	Illustrated by Nicolas Mordvinoff Written by William Lipkind
1951	**The Egg Tree** (Scribner)	Katherine Mulhouse
1950	**Song of the Swallows** (Scribner)	Leo Politi
1949	**The Big Snow** (Macmillan)	Berra & Elmer Hade
1948	**White Snow, Bright Snow** (Lothrop)	Illustrated by Roger Duvoisin Written by Alvin Tresselt
1947	**The Little Island** (Doubleday)	Illustrated by Leonard Weisgard Written by Golden MacDonald
1946	**The Rooster Crows** (Macmillan)	Maude & Miska Petersham
1945	**Prayer for a Child** (Macmillan)	Illustrated by Elizabeth Orton Jones Written by Rachel Field
1944	**Many Moons** (Harcourt)	Illustrated by Louis Slobodkin Written by James Thurber
1943	**The Little House** (Houghton)	Virginia Lee Burton
1942	**Make Way for Ducklings** (Viking)	Robert McCloskey
1941	**They Were Strong and Good** (Viking)	Robert Lawson
1940	**Abraham Lincoln** (Doubleday)	Ingri & Edgar Parin d'Aulaire
1939	**Mei Li** (Doubleday)	Thomas Handforth
1938	**Animals of the Bible, A Picture Book** (Lippincott)	Illustrated by Dorothy P. Lathrop Written by Helen Dean Fish

Appendix B

Additional Resources

Children's Literature Websites

American Library Association
http://www.ala.org
Official site of the American Library Association. Contains many links for information on children's literature, including the following:

Book Lists from the Young Adult Library Service
http://www.ala.org/alsc/notable97.html

Book Links: Connecting Books, Libraries, and Classrooms
http://www.ala.org/BookLinks

Association for Library Service to Children (ALSC)
http://www.ala.org/alsc
American Library Association committee specializing in library services for children. Contains many links to other sites that feature literature and learning activities.

The Bulletin of the Center for Children's Books
http://edfu.lis.uiuc.edu/puboff/bccb
Web page of The Bulletin of the Center for Children's Books, a children's book review journal.

CBC Online
http://www.cbcbooks.org
Children's Book Council Web page. This Web page is devoted to the many aspects of children's literature

Carol Hurst's Children's Literature
http://www.carolhurst.com
Includes curriculum support for literature and book reviews. Has good ideas for incorporating good literature in the school curriculum.

Child_Lit
http://www.rci.rutgers.edu/~mjoseph/childlit/about.html
An online discussion list for those interested in the research and theory of children's literature and its use with children. Postings are from librarians, teachers, parents, authors and professors.

Additional Resources

Child Study Children's Book Committee

http://www.bnkst.edu

A World Wide Web site maintained by the Child Study Children's Book Committee at Bank Street College. This site contains useful information pertaining to the study of children and their books.

Children's Literature Authors & Illustrators

http://www.ucet.ufl.edu/%7Ejbrown/chauth.html

Internet sites for numerous children's authors and illustrators.

Children's Literature & Language Arts Resources

http://falcon.jmu.edu/~ramseyil/childlit.htm

Maintained by James Madison University, this site contains links for book reviews, educational sites, and numerous genre in children's literature.

Children's Literature Association

http://ebbs.english.vt.edu/chla

Neat site with nice information. This Association is devoted to the scholarly study of children's literature, and it offers links to other sites on this subject.

Children's Literature Homepage

http://www.childrenslit.com

Contains information on children's literature and book reviews. The book reviews are written by librarians, teacher and parents.

Children's Literature Reference

http://www.lib.utexas.edu/Libs/PCL/child

Contains excellent links for children's literature, and is an electronic bibliography of children's reference resources. This site can be used as a guide for students and researchers to basic and special resources on children's literature.

Children's Literature Web Guide

http://www.ucalgary.ca/~dkbrown/

An excellent guide to Internet resources dealing with children's literature. This site contains many links, and is one of the most comprehensive sites for the study and enjoyment of children and their books. The Guide is kept current and timely.

Database of Award-Winning Children's Literature

http://www2.wcoil.com/~ellerbee/childlit.html

A site in which you can choose the specific type of award winning children's book you desire. The author of this Internet resource is a librarian with an interest in children's literature.

The deGrummond Children's Literature Collection

http://www.lib.usm.edu/~degrum

A children's literature research center, housed at the University of Southern Mississippi. The deGrummond Collection houses an Ezra Jack Keats collection.

Digital Librarian: Children's Literature

http://www.servtech.com/~mvail/childlit.html

A large "webliography" of links for children's literature subjects. This site is a good site for all who use children's literature in education.

Index to Internet Sites: Children's and Young Adults' Authors & Illustrators

http://falcon.jmu.edu/schoollibrary/biochildhome.htm

Part of the Internet School Library Media Center, this exhaustive site lists numerous children's authors and book illustrators.

Inez Ramsey's Kids Sites: Meet the Author

http://falcon.jmu.edu/schoollibrary/kidsauthors.htm

A list of links for children's authors on the World Wide Web. This site is part of the Internet School Library Media Center.

The Internet Public Library

http://www.ipl.org

A good resource that includes a children's literature section, with information on children's books and a "story-time."

Links for Book Lovers

http://home.sprynet.com/sprynet/balgassi/links.htm

A great page featuring author links, publishers and online bookstores.

Vandergrift's Children's Literature Page

http://www.scils.rutgers.edu/special/kay/childlit.html

An extensive site developed by Kay E. Vandergrift at Rutgers University. This site is continually evolving and contains excellent research on children's literature.

Yahoo! - Arts:Humanitites: Literature: Genres: Children's: Authors

http://www.yahoo.com/Arts/Humanities/Literature/Genres/Children_s/Authors

Links for various authors of children's books.

Educational Materials Websites

American Library Association

http://www.ala.org

Official site of the American Library Association. Contains many links for educational information, including the following:

ALA Resources for Parents and Kids

http://www.ala.org/parents/

700+ Great Sites

http://www.ala.org/parentspage/greatsites/amazing.html

Additional Resources

700+ Great Sites - Library and School Sites
http://www.ala.org/parentspage/greatsites/lib.html

For Parent and Caregivers
http://www.ala.org/alsc/parents.links.html

Learning Through the Library
http://www.ala.org/aasl/learning/

Produced by the American Association of School Librarians (AASL), this site features a best practices site, and links to learning. The AASL is a component of the American Library Association.

AskEric
http://ericir.syr.edu

Maintained by the ERIC clearinghouse for educational information. Includes many excellent and useful literature based lesson plans suitable for classroom use.

Awesome Library
http://www.neat-schoolhouse.org/awesome.html

This site features over 12,000 links for teachers, parents, librarians, and kids. An excellent resource of information.

Blue Web'n Learning Sites Library
http://www.kn.pacbell.com/wired/bluewebn

Educational learning on the Web. Sponsored by Pacific Bell, this site links to other "Blue Ribbon" sites offering curriculum resources and activities.

Classroom Connect
http://www.classroom.net

This site offers activities and product news for teachers and their students in graded K –12.

Early Childhood Resources
http://www.monroe.k12.la.us/mcs/community/early_child/early_child.html

Numerous links designed for use with the youngest children are included in this website. A good resource for teachers, librarians and parents.

Education Place
http://www.eduplace.com

Presented by Houghton Mifflin Publishers, this site offers resources for teachers and parents, as well as a "Kid's Clubhouse" with educational games and activities.

Education World
http://www.education-world.com

Featured at this site is information for all areas of education including administration, books in education, curriculum, and lesson planning. This site features a searchable database of over 110,000 Web pages.

Free Online Unit Studies

http://www.alaska.net/~cccandc/free.htm

A database of lessons developed with the Internet in mind. These lessons can be used in public, private or homeschool settings.

The Global Schoolhouse

http://www.gsn.org

The Global Schoolhouse features sections for parents and teachers, kids and teens and a link for neat projects. The parent/teacher section offers information on discussion lists, resources and tools and K-12 educational opportunities.

ICONnect

http://ala.org/ICONN/index.html

A site for curriculum connections and Internet resources, maintained by the American Library Association.

Internet in the Classroom

http://129.120.20.20/rhondac/classrm.html

Includes curriculum resources, online classrooms, teacher resource sites, professional development and an area for children. A good site to illustrate the variety of ways the Internet can be used in the classroom.

Internet School Library Media Center

http://falcon.jmu.edu/schoollibrary/index.html

School librarians and teachers will gain valuable insight from this Web page. Listed are resources for various elementary curriculum areas, professional organizations and special education.

The Internet Schoolhouse

http://www.onr.com/schoolhouse/is.html

A neat site with numerous links for all types of educational curriculum needs. This site is fun to navigate, as the main menu is a "highway" with many exits.

Kathy Schrock's Guide for Educators

http://school.discovery.com/schrockguide

A useful educational site, loaded with many links. The categorized list of sites on the Internet are useful for enhancing curriculum and teacher professional growth. Kathy Schrock's Guide for Educators is an excellent site for those interested in the education of children.

The Mailbox

http://www.learningmagazine.com/mailbox/mbxhome.html

The home page for "The Mailbox" educational magazine, this site features a preview of upcoming issues and links for free educational samples.

Mustang: A Web Cruising Vehicle for Teachers

http://mustang.coled.umn.edu

From the University of Minnesota. This site simplifies searching the Web for educational resources.

SCORE: CyberGuides

http://www.sdcoe.k12.ca.us/score/cyberguide.html

Includes teacher guides and student activities for literature on the Internet. Sponsored by School of California, Online Resources for Education (SCORE).

TeacherLINK

http://www.teacherlink.usu.edu/TLresources.html

Includes links to educational Web pages, lesson plans, curriculum extenders and subject area links. TeacherLINKS is provided by the Utah State University College of Education.

Teachers.Net

http://www.teachers.net

Chat center, lessons. reference resources, websites and networking opportunities for educators.

Books

Other useful tools for discovering information about the Internet are the following books. This bibliography is a short version of selected works that are available in many libraries or bookstores.

Benson, Allen C., and Linda M.Fodemski. **Connecting Kids and the Internet: A Handbook for Librarians, Teachers, and Parents**. Neal-Schuman, 1996. An extensive and useful reference. *Connecting Kids and the Internet* is a useful guide for all adults.

Campbell, Hope. **Teaching Language Arts With the Internet: Internet Lesson Plans and Classroom Activities**. Classroom Connect, 1997. A wealth of ideas for classroom use. Classroom Connect is known for its resources on the World Wide Web at http://www.classroom.net.

Dinsmore, Mark & Wendy. **Homeschool guide to the Internet: Your Onramp to the Information Superhighway.** Homeschool Press, 1996. A useful tool for all education situations that contains more than 250 resources. Those in public and private schools and libraries will find the information useful as well.

Kehoe, Brendan P. **Children and the Internet: A Zen Guide for Parents and Educators.** Prentice Hall, 1997. Internet basics for adults interested in the use of the Web with children. The information presented is clear and understandable.

Lamb, Annette C. **Building Treehouses for Learning: Technology in Today's Classroom.** Vision to Action, 1997. Planning effective lessons for the technology classroom.

Offutt, Elizabeth Rhodes. **Internet Without Fear: Practical Tips and Activities for the Elementary Classroom.** Good Apple, 1996. From the publisher of *The Good Apple* educational journal. This book would be a good book for all interested in using the Internet in the classroom.

Pedersen, Ted, and Francis Moss. ***Internet for Kids: A Beginners's Guide to Surfin the Net.*** Price Stern Sloan, 1997. An updated version that includes a parents' and teachers' guide. Good for use in the classroom with children to aid in understanding how to search the World Wide Web.

Schrock, Kathleen. ***Evaluating Internet Web Sites: An Educator's Guide.*** Master Teacher, 1997. From the author of the acclaimed educational website, this book is a good resource for the educator and parent.

LearningQuest Template

Your LearningQuest Title Here

<u>Introduction</u>   <u>Assignment</u>   <u>Internet Resources</u>   <u>Activities</u>   <u>Fun Things to Do</u>

<u>Conclusion</u>

Introduction

State an introduction to your Learning-Quest in this space.

Assignment

You can write your task as a paragraph or in a bulleted list. The paragraph can describe the outcomes which will be attained following the completion of the LearningQuest.

- If you wish to use a bulleted list, begin here with the first step.
- Step #2.
- Continue as necessary to complete the steps for your Learning-Quest.

Internet Resources

Information about the resources the learner will use can be written here.

- <u>Link Title</u>. Describe the link to clarify if you wish. Clarify which question(s) this URL will address.
- <u>Link Title</u>. Description. Question(s)
- <u>Link Title</u>. Description. Question(s)

Activities

1. List the questions or activities which will be completed during the LearningQuest.

2. Additional questions/activities.

3. Continue or delete as required to meet objectives to answer questions or provide activities to reinforce leaning during the LearningQuest.

Fun Things to Do

This space can extend the learning process through additional activities, Internet sites or ideas. Children can draw pictures based on what they learned, complete an Internet activity or numerous other education activities.

Conclusion

A summarization of the learning can be placed here. You can also place some additional resources or Internet addresses in this space.

This page maintained by (Your name). Written, (mm/dd/yy). Last updated, mm/dd/yy.

This page adapted from the LearningQuest template written by Ru Story-Huffman, based on the WebQuest concept developed by Bernie Dodge.

LearningQuest Template With HTML Coding

<HTML> ←———————————

<HEAD>

<TITLE>*LearningQuest Template*</TITLE>

</HEAD>

<BODY BGCOLOR ="#ffffff">

<A NAME="Top">

<B>*Your LearningQuest Title Here*</B>

<HR><B>

<A HREF="#Introduction">Introduction</A>

<A HREF="#Assignment">Assignment</A>

<A HREF="#Internet Resources">Internet Resources</A>

<A HREF="#Questions">Questions</A>

<A HREF="#Learning Advice">Learning Advice</A>

<A HREF="#Conclusion">Conclusion</A>

<P><B><A NAME="Introduction">Introduction</A></B>

<P>*State an introduction to your LearningQuest in this space.*

<P><B><A NAME="Assignment">Assignment</A></B>

<P>*You can write your task as a paragraph or in a bulleted list. The paragraph can describe the outcomes which will be attained following the completion of the LearningQuest.*<UL>

<LI>*If you wish to use a bulleted list, begin here with the first step.*

<LI>*Step #2.*

<LI>*Step #3.*

<LI>*Continue as necessary to complete the steps for your LearningQuest.*</UL>

<P><B><A NAME="Internet Resources">Internet Resources</A></B>

<P>*Information about the resources the learner will use can be written here.*<UL>

<LI><a href="*Place full URL here*">*Place web page name here*</a>
Description (Describe the link to clarify if you wish.) Question(s) (Clarify which question(s) this URL will address.)

> Start your document here. If you do not have Web authoring software, a text only document with an .htm extension will work.

<LI><a href="*Place full URL here*">*Place web page name here*</a>
Description. Question(s)

<LI><a href="*Place full URL here*">*Place web page name here*</a>
Description. Question(s)

<P><B><A NAME="Questions">Questions</A><OL></B>

<LI>*List the questions which will be answered at the completion of the LearningQuest.*

<LI>*Additional questions.*

<LI>*Continue or delete as required to meet objectives to answer questions for the LearningQuest.*</OL>

<P><B><A NAME="Learning Advice">Learning Advice</A></B>

<P>*This space can be used to provide help for the students for use as they explore the Internet using the LearningQuest.*

<P><B><A NAME="Conclusion">Conclusion</A></B>

<P>*A summarization of the learning can be placed here. You can also place some additional resources or Internet addresses in this space.*

<HR>This page maintained by *(Your name)*. Written, *(mm/dd/yy)*. Last updated, *(mm/dd/yy)*. http://www.*yourURL*/ *YourDocumentName*.htm</B>

<A HREF="#Top"> Top of Page

</BODY>

</HTML> ← This should be the last element in your document.

Note: Italics indicate where your text should be placed. Use plain text for your inserted information, italics are here only to indicate where new text should be added.

When you have finished your LearningQuest, you can test it in your Web browser. If you do not have Web authoring software, select the Open File option from the File pulldown menu. Different browsers will render type differently. If you are using LearningQuests on a single type of computer with one browser you can get more creative with type and graphics without losing control of the way your document appears on screen.

You can also find an electronic version of this template at:

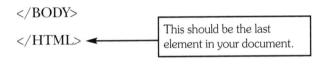 **Link** for *Caldecott on the Net*
www.hpress.highsmith.com/rsh1up.htm